OUTSMARTING
REALITY

Nero Knowledge

TABLE OF CONTENTS

A WORD TO THE READER

I am typically hired by elite six to eight figure entrepreneurs, professional athletes, and Hollywood actors.

Not for what they publicly preach about "hard work" or "smart strategies."

But for what they will never tell you the hidden, esoteric, and metaphysical secrets of the universe that allow them to achieve more by doing less.

I am brought in to help them transcend effort entirely.

To show them how to operate multi-dimensionally where it is no longer about working harder or even smarter but about stepping into a state where the universe itself seems to be on your side.

Where results flow effortlessly from alignment, not force.

My clients have doubled, tripled, even quadrupled their revenue in weeks, landed TV roles, and accelerated their careers not by working harder or doing more, but by shifting their beliefs and aligning with the success they once chased.

This is the real secret behind many of the world's elites.

It is not that they are intentionally hiding it from the world.

The truth is, even if they did speak of it openly, most people would dismiss it because it defies the logic and beliefs that society is conditioned to accept.

In a way, through this book, *you* have hired me, and for that, I thank you. I have not held back at all.

It's an honour, and truly, a pleasure to share with you the knowledge usually reserved for those at the top.

However, it must be made clear that this book will do no more for you than you allow it to.

You will find no more in these pages than you allow yourself to find.

Decide that this book will position you to alter your reality for the rest of your life, and you will position yourself to do so.

Decide that you will experience lightbulb moments while reading this book and let your mind light up.

Decide that this book will be more than enough for things to change, and change will come.

FOREWORD

WRITTEN BY MAMA NERO

When my mother was a little girl, it was her dream to be an author.

I wish to make that dream come true, so I asked her to write my foreword.

Thank you, mama:

I stood motionless for a moment, clutching the worn-out broom in my hand.

My thoughts were far away. I stared intently at one spot near the ragged fence that separated our yard from the neighbour's. I vaguely took in the ailing hedge that had not quite prospered in its duty to provide added security and privacy to us.

What occupied my thoughts was an image of me living abroad. I saw myself working hard to support my family.

My thoughts spun around to what my father had said a while ago he told me that the only way our family's life could improve was if he were dead, then we could do whatever we thought was best to improve our lot.

I clutched the broom tighter due to an intense feeling of frustration and felt the dried grass digging into my hand. With determination, I started sweeping the leaves away.

I continued this motion, my back bent, until the small area in front of the house was clean. All the while, my thoughts had transported me to an unknown land, far, far away from here.

I knew back then that I was going to make it there was no doubt in my mind. I was going to be the one to take my family out of poverty.

My father was a government worker, with a relatively good salary. My mother was a homemaker. However, despite my father's job, daily life was a struggle.

I could feel my mother's unhappiness like a sharp knife in my side. I saw her struggling to raise us children, trying to make ends meet.

I saw her pain after my youngest brother was born. She suffered from a mysterious illness that left me fearful she was going to die.

I was nine years old at the time, living in fear every day that the one person who struggled daily for our wellbeing might not make it.

I started to pay more and more attention to her. I realised at that young age that she was suffering. In the tiny home we lived in, it wasn't difficult to overhear the adults talking — arguing about money, school fees, and daily living expenses.

Daydreaming became my escape. I started to imagine a better life than the one I was in; a life where I could provide a safe, loving home for my family, where all basic necessities were met, and money was plentiful. This led me to dream vividly about being a millionaire.

Thus, my childhood was spent watching my mother's face daily, trying to gauge the level of stress she was under, feeling powerless in the face of her misery.

I vowed not to be a source of added stress for her. I began hiding anything I thought might cause her worry.

When my shoes were torn, I would sit quietly in the corner and mend them with pieces of twine I had picked up near the tree where the shoe mender waited for customers.

My source of joy became escaping to the only place no one else in the world could penetrate: a corner of my mind where everything was as it should be.

My mother was happy, safe, and free from worry about the next meal, school fees, rent, or other basic needs.

In that space, I could give her money freely, so she didn't have to worry about anything. I imagined her having more money than the so-called "educated" woman my father constantly compared her to.

My mother's words constantly rang in my ears. She told me I could be more, do more, and most importantly, to never settle like she did. She always emphasised the importance of having a certificate in my own name.

When I passed my GCSE exams, my uncle who lived abroad sent me a cheque for what was a substantial amount at the time, as a way of congratulating me.

I knew the money would solve a few immediate problems, but I wanted more than a handout. I dreamed of a job that could truly change our lives.

I persisted in my vivid daydreams, seeing myself living abroad, sending money home to my mother, helping with bills, and paying my brother's school fees.

I never cashed that cheque. Instead, I held onto it as a symbol of hope proof that I could escape this life.

My intuition told me my uncle was going to be my way out.

My imaginings became more focused, more realistic. I could feel the tension in my spirit as the realisation dawned that my dreams could come true. I could feel it in my bones.

I withdrew into myself more and more, spending time alone with my thoughts imagining my uncle sending for me to join his family in the UK. I felt immense joy from this exercise.

This escape into my secret world became a daily routine. I used every opportunity, especially during solitary chores, to visit that wonderful life where I was able to solve all my family's financial needs.

Then, one day after I had written my GCSE examinations and had started working as a shop assistant in a local shopping centre, news came from my uncle. He was going to send an air ticket for me to attend university in the United Kingdom.

When I heard the news, I wasn't surprised. There was no ecstatic moment of joy: what I had been waiting for had finally happened.

I hastily sent a message to my school friends to say I was travelling, then went to the capital city and arranged for a passport, which came through in a few days. Within weeks, I was in the UK.

It wasn't until years later, when my son became my teacher, that I realised what had truly happened. I had a burning, overwhelming desire to succeed. That desire led me to create and cross a bridge of incidents that caused my dream to manifest into reality.

Somehow, my untrained mind had caused a shift in the universe, prompting my uncle and his wife to make arrangements for me to join them, making my desires come true.

In a new and foreign land, I started working toward my goals barely an adult, but already taking on responsibilities within my family, just as I had promised myself I would.

Then my son was born, before I had even completed my nursing education. My family was disappointed in me, seeing it as a failure. But I remembered my mother's words how her own family had seen no value in educating her simply because she was a girl. They believed she would just get married and never benefit the family.

I became even more determined. I completed my course while my family cared for my son. Now, I had a more pressing reason to work hard to get my child back from the parents I had entrusted him to.

Over the next 20 years, I stopped listening to that inner voice of my childhood. I lost the directions to that tiny room in the corner of my mind that I used to escape to.

I told myself I had no time for childish fancies. I became more concerned with surviving, solving other people's problems ahead of my own, and most importantly, being a good mother to my son, Nero.

Occasionally, I would think back to that time when I held the broom in my hand, pressing hard on it while daydreaming only to have my strongest desire come true.

That moment became a reminder of what I could achieve with my thoughts alone and a strong desire.

My greatest joy growing up was bending reality. I could escape to far and amazing worlds simply by opening a book and losing myself in it. I wanted my son to experience this wondrous world too. I started encouraging him to read, for fun.

Imagine my joy when he asked me to buy him books. That joy soon turned to mild concern when I noticed the titles he was drawn to.

My son began an adventure of a lifetime. Before I knew it, he was devouring books daily, asking for one after another, all while completing his education.

Even as I tried to guide him, I sensed that his energy was greater than mine. I had lived in survival mode; he did not.

I became curious about the books he was reading, wondering how his mind worked, slightly perplexed by this person in front of me. Then I tried reading the books myself... and I couldn't understand a thing.

Then the haze began to lift, and I started thinking again. I tried to reconnect with that part of my mind that could make the unseen real.

I am currently working through the fear of who and what I can become if I once again apply myself and harness the power of my mind, as that young girl once did.

I walk through the maze daily, with my teacher Nero holding my hand.

Having learned that before I can change anyone else, I must first change myself; I continue my onward journey of self-discovery.

I am forever a student of the universe, learning its laws and its secrets with the belief that I can partake in the banquet that is laid out before me.

> *"Say not ye, There are yet four months, and then cometh harvest? Behold, I say unto you, Lift up your eyes, and look on the fields; for they are white already to harvest."*
> **John 4:35**

Seeing things that are not yet seen as if they were seen has been the biggest lesson so far. For everything, every circumstance, starts off as a thought and becomes visible for all to see.

Happy learning, reader.

INTRODUCTION

Outsmarting reality is like a game of chess in which you are outsmarting your old frequency.

At first glance the title of this book raises a lot of questions:

What does it mean to outsmart reality?

Can I outsmart reality?

How do I outsmart reality?

Why do I need to outsmart reality?

What will I get from outsmarting reality?

It may seem like something completely audacious that is beyond you. However, that is only if you're not operating from your true self.

The truth is, outsmarting reality is the only way you will create your desired reality.

If you cannot outsmart reality, then you will always feel like you are step behind where you want to be in life, which I assume is already how you feel.

Unfortunately, this is how the masses live, forever wishing they were in another reality, without realising that they are simply losing a game for which they weren't given the rules.

Imagine playing a game of chess without knowing how all the pieces move.

Whether you realise this or not, there is another version of you that you spiritually created that desires nothing more than to remain the same at any cost, even to your own detriment.

The word "reality" may be in the title of this book, but the truth is, it's just you.

Until you can make sense of you, then nothing in your reality will make sense, for reality is no more than what you are.

You and your reality are one; there is no separation between you, but the unawareness of this unity is the source of your disharmony.

The book isn't even about reality. No form of manifestation should ever be about reality, or changing the world. It's about the only thing that matters – and that is you.

That brings me to the sole purpose of this book, which is to get you to give yourself your desired reality before the world gives it to you.

Whatever it is you desire to be in this life, you need to become it before the world proves it to you. I don't believe you should be worried about enlightenment, opening your third eye, ancient civilisations, the true origin of humanity, bloodlines, 5G and psychic abilities if you're struggling to pay your bills or worse, wishing your reality was different.

Now, it may not be that extreme for you, but the basic premise of this book is, if you're not in your desired reality then what is the point?

With all due disrespect, you have bigger concerns, and those concerns revolve around actually living in a reality that you want.

Don't get me wrong, those things have their place most definitely, but spirituality without the ability to control your reality is nothing but complete vanity.

I repeat, the only aim of this book is to get you to give yourself your desired reality.

With that being said, I'd also like to clarify that you won't find any sexy new techniques, strategies or methods for "manifesting" in this book, and I put that in quotes because it's likely you have the wrong definition of what that even means.

The only things you will find are timeless principles that explain the mechanics of the universe in relation to creation and how it/you work.

The final thing I'd like to make clear is that you may be holding a book, but that's not what you're reading; what you are reading is your level of consciousness and nothing more.

The reason for that is, you don't see reality as it is; you only see it as you are, and you are forever evolving, forever changing, so what is revealed to you today won't be the same as next week.

This book will not be your saviour; you are your only saviour.

THE OLD FREQUENCY

PRINCIPLE

Your old frequency will forever be the only thing that holds you back from your new frequency and, as a result, your new reality.

The moment you begin the journey of creating your desired reality, you threaten the existence of something you never knew existed.

And that is your old frequency.

Your old frequency is a living entity, with its own psychology and its own goals. So long as you are unaware of how it thinks, you will always be a step behind it, unconsciously driven towards its goals without realising.

Its only goal is to keep you within the old reality, the one that you are seeking to escape.

All those times when it felt like your life was spiralling out of control, it was always in your control – but unfortunately in the control of your old frequency.

Before we dive into the psychology and the goals of the old frequency, it's important you understand how it came into existence.

The easiest way to think about your old frequency is as your doppelganger existing on the spiritual plane.

An identical version of you, with all your memories, all your beliefs, all your experiences, all your feelings; just with its own version of your memories, its own version of your beliefs, its own version of your experiences and its own version of your feelings.

It doesn't exist physically as you do because it resides in the spiritual plane, hence why it has the ability to affect your reality because before anything can exist physically it must exist vibrationally.

Unfortunately, since to the ego anything that cannot be seen does not exist, the old frequency often damages your reality without you ever even knowing.

It is created out of what is called thought-forms. The easiest way to conceptualise thought-forms is to see them as stones representing mental and emotional energy.

Imagine that every time you repeat a particular line of thinking or feel a particular emotion, a stone is placed on the ground, forming a pile. Studies have shown the average person has anywhere from 6,000 to 60,000 thoughts a day. Over time, those piles turn into mountains.

Every repeated thought and emotion are a building block in the creation of an entity that will seek to exist based on what it was made from.

A couple of examples should highlight this more clearly:

Take the person who repeatedly complains they are "unlucky."

Life doesn't go their way, and they think to themselves: *Why me; why always me?*

(Note that the idea of life not going your way is an illusion; life is always going your way, you're just unaware of your path.)

This repeated mental and emotional energy creates an entity. Guess what that entity's goal is? To make them unlucky!

It's natural for us to wonder why the mind would do this.

Does it hate me?

Why is it trying to ruin my life?

The entities we create are like giving birth to a blind intelligence. It is made by us and becomes addicted to the thoughts and emotions it is breastfed.

In the instance of the "unlucky" individual, the emotions that made and breastfed the entity were frustration, irritation, anger, apathy, sadness and depletion.

The entity is like a spiritual parasite.

It sustains itself by feeding off the emotions that created it, so it will sway the events of your reality to generate those emotions within you even if this leads to your own destruction.

It's important not to become annoyed by the entity. After all, it is of your own making and is blindly operating from the intelligence given to it by you.

What the mind has done, it can undo, no matter the reality.

Within this third-dimensional realm, we are subject to the law of polarity, the concept that everything exists has its energetic opposite. Here are some of the most common examples:

Masculine – Feminine

Negative – Positive

Rich – Poor

Lucky – Unlucky

If someone can create negative entities that contradict their desired reality, they can just as easily create positive entities that contribute towards their desired reality.

Some people are regarded as "lucky." Life always seems to bend to their will and things always goes right for them. These individuals simply exist with an entity that seeks to keep them "lucky" and feeds off their joy, happiness, and amazement!

A close friend of mine, who grew up believing she wasn't good looking, eventually decided to see herself as the most beautiful woman ever.

Now, wherever she goes, men are constantly chasing her, approaching her and eager to do anything for her.

Whether she realises it or not, she's created an energetic presence: an entity that influences how others perceive her.

This entity is sustained by the thoughts and emotions she holds about herself, and in turn, it reflects those beliefs back through the way others respond to her.

As you go through life, you're going to have many different phases, and in every one an entity is created that will seek to maintain that phase.

If you're financially struggling, there is an entity that seeks to maintain that.

If you're in a bad relationship, there is an entity that seeks to maintain that.

If you're unfit, there is an entity that seeks to maintain that.

The old frequency is directly connected with the old version of you, which is directly connected with the old reality – the very one you're trying to escape.

Until you know how your old frequency thinks, you will be a step behind it every time without ever knowing why. Understanding its aim is imperative.

The goal of the old frequency is simple, and that is to exist.

The old version of you will stop at nothing, even if it means your destruction and total misery, to shift from the spiritual to material. Ultimately, like other spirits or entities, it wants to become one with your reality.

I can't emphasise this enough: it will do whatever takes.

Now we have defined its aim, let's shift our focus to its psychology, which has four main characteristics.

These qualities are nothing more than a humanistic conceptualisation meant to provide a more relatable, simple understanding.

1. Needy

To put it quite simply, the old version of you is an attention seeker. It is desperate for your attention.

Where attention goes, energy flows. If the old version of you can capture your attention, even if only temporarily, it has opened the door to get back in.

Concentration precedes vibration, vibration precedes frequency and frequency precedes reality. Through your attention it can nourish itself.

Focus is a centralisation of energy, and the old version of you knows this so it will sway events, circumstances, conditions and even people in your reality to reflect the old reality, all to get you to redirect your energy towards it, specifically your emotional energy.

Emotion is energy, so it'll always seek to extract it in a manner reflective of what you've got it accustomed to. The old frequency must feed, and it will do so at any cost.

It is needy because it's been with you during all the low moments of your life whether you knew it or not, even though it was feeding off you. It is the best friend that occasionally ruins your life.

2. Sadistic

The old version of you is a sadist.

It loves pain, sadness, frustration, irritation and annoyance because that's the energy it feeds off. It rejoices in your suffering and all the very emotions you're attempting to leave behind.

It's likely that during times of adversity these are the predominant emotions occupying you, which are like a drug to the old frequency. It sustains itself with them.

Remember, too, that emotions act as a glue that sticks you to the old frequency, ultimately binding you to your old reality.

The old version of you *is* you, so it knows exactly which buttons to press to trigger the emotions it craves.

The moment you start feeling too calm, too peaceful or begin shifting toward a new reality, that's when it strikes.

It's not random; it's a calculated pullback, designed to stir up the most emotional resistance possible and keep you anchored in the familiar so the idea of change seems like a hopeless dream.

3. Scared

The old version of you likes existing, so the thought of not existing frightens it, and ultimately this is the beginning of a trap which captures many of us.

Sensing its own potential extinction, the old version of you will project its fear onto you the moment you begin striving for more or moving in a new direction.

As you shift into the frequency of your desired reality, it attempts to make you unconsciously associate that change with fear so you'll hesitate, retreat or self-sabotage.

It's a defence mechanism, designed to keep you tethered to the familiar and prevent your evolution into a better reality.

It also knows that once you feel fear, it's only a matter of time before that fear begins to negatively alter your frequency since fear is nothing more than ignorant faith, which then eventually alters your reality.

Fear is like a guiding light for what you don't want to navigate the universe so it can find you.

Due to the emotional strength of fear, it ultimately overshadows the frequency sent out for your desired reality, taking over to manifest the worst.

That fear of change is not yours; it belongs to the old frequency, which tricks you into thinking it's yours so you don't move forward.

4. Reactive

The old version of you is extremely reactive, but the irony is that it is reactive to its own creation. Once again, this is the beginning of a very dangerous but calculated cycle.

Since the old version of you is in opposition to the creation of your desired reality, it will cause adversity in your reality while also short-circuiting your thinking to shut down the potential of any higher levels of awareness, which is seeing reality clearly beyond illusion.

It ultimately doesn't want you to be aware of the true nature of reality and what is going on.

It wants you to be caught up in the whirlwind of chaos so you never become aware, because all transmutation first begins with awareness.

It'll project its tendency to quickly react to circumstances, conditions, events, and people so there is no time for awareness, so there is no transmutation.

It's important to note that emotion is the most powerful energy source in the universe, and so the old version will seek an emotional reaction from you; that is all it wants.

Every time you emotionally react, you are strengthening and reinforcing the old frequency. Emotion is a supercharger of frequency, and so you are supercharging the old reality.

Always remember, on the car journey to your desired reality, emotionally reacting to the old version of you, and ultimately the old reality, will take you on a detour back to it.

PRACTICAL

Awareness is the only way you'll escape the clutches of your old frequency. The moment you are aware, a pathway that was once hidden opens itself up, giving you the option to live by design instead of default.

Within the adversity that reality presents to you, there is a choice, and that is to live by default or design.

Default pertains to the old frequency that expects you to react.

Reacting to reality will always lead to the old frequency.

Design pertains to the new frequency that expects you to respond.

Responding to reality will always lead to the new frequency.

The difference between reacting and responding is life and death.

Reacting is death, and responding is life.

To rise to your desired reality, you must rise above reaction into response.

Let's examine how the old frequency perceives reacting.

Reacting is to allow the external nature of reality to imbalance your internal state.

You've been wired to think that you react to reality, but the truth is reality reacts to you.

The internal is a reflector. So, ironically, once it is swayed it will lead to the swaying of the external, and this is the beginning of a cycle in which too many are trapped.

To simplify the point being made here, an imbalance of the internal creates everything you don't like.

By responding instead of reacting, you allow your internal state to balance the external nature of reality.

Internal balance ultimately leads to a balanced reality no matter what is presented.

Responding is simply the act of viewing your current adversity through the lens of your desired reality, reframing the situation to be in alignment with where you're going, not where you are.

How would the version of you in your desired reality look at this?

How would the version of you in your desired reality feel about this?

How would the version of you in your desired reality think about this?

If you can keep those questions at the top of your mind while experiencing adversity, the blur on your lenses caused by that chaos will begin to clear.

REALITY DOESN'T CARE
IF YOU'RE NICE

PRINCIPLE

Why do bad things happen to good people?

Why do people with the biggest hearts suffer the most?

What of justice?

We all wish we lived in a world where God rewarded the good and punished the evil, but a quick look around shows the opposite to be true. Denial of this truth is nothing more than cognitive dissonance.

To most of us, it just doesn't make sense, and that's because we're making the mistake of thinking like a human instead of thinking like the universe.

The universe itself is nothing more than a system, a collection of laws that operate indiscriminately to humans.

To say it more simply, when it comes to the reality that you create, the universe doesn't care if you're good or bad.

The universe is unapologetically equal to all, regardless of age, regardless of circumstance and, unfortunately, regardless of morality.

When it comes to reality, the only thing the universe registers is frequency or the state of consciousness that you are occupying. This constructs the world you live in.

This unfortunate spiritual truth seems somewhat disheartening, but remember that "spiritual" itself means beyond the physical.

It refers to beyond the third-dimensional realm, which means beyond all constructs within it such as morality, ultimately meaning they do not apply.

Morality is a human construct that has been spiritualised and commercialised to make us think that being good people entitles us to the reward of a good life. It should, but it doesn't.

You need to stop thinking like a human and more like the universe. To do so, you must observe how the universe actually operates rather than how you think it should.

The laws and energy of the universe highlight as clear as day the bittersweet truth that we delude ourselves.

Fire will treat the good and the evil the same.

Rain will treat the good and the evil the same.

Gravity will treat the good and the evil the same.

Electricity will treat the good and the evil the same.

Now apply this to the law of creation: whatever frequency you emit will be reflected; whatever your state of consciousness will be materialised; whatever is within will eventually be without.

The universe has never hidden how it works from us. Through our own cognitive dissonance, we've hidden how it works from ourselves, preferring to cling to the illusion of a cosmic justice without realising the universe interprets justice as frequency, and it will never lie to you.

To be clear, I do not want to live in a world without morals, respect and integrity. Morality must exist for society to run harmoniously, but it is not enough to be a good person.

The universe doesn't reward good people. It rewards those who reward themselves with a frequency which complements their desired reality; no more, no less.

The true issue here isn't how the universe operates, but how we've been taught it does.

Most of us were raised with the idea that if we do good, we will experience good. But life happens and confusion hits.

We do good deeds, we help others, we show love and kindness but we still suffer …

You can have good morals, but with a bad mind, badness will be created every time.

You can have bad morals, but with a good mind, goodness will be created every time.

There's nothing wrong with being a good person. In fact, it should be encouraged. But don't think for a second that being a good person qualifies you for your desired reality.

The only thing that qualifies you for your desired reality is the frequency of your desired reality.

It seems as if the nicest people often have the worst frequencies, ultimately creating the worst realities.

They are riddled with low confidence, low self-belief, doubt, fear, worries and stresses without realising each one of those components contribute to a frequency that corresponds to a reality of nothing but suffering, struggle, failure, misery and misfortune.

On the other hand, it seems as if the most evil people often have the best frequencies, ultimately creating the best realities.

They are brimming with iron-clad confidence, self-belief, conviction, certainty and power without realising each one of those components contribute to a frequency that corresponds to a reality of nothing but success, power, prosperity, peace and fortune.

How often do we admire powerful, successful people in society, overlooking their unpleasant or immoral ways as we wallow in our virtues and suffering?

The conclusion often mistakenly made is that success is directly intertwined with evil, and those who are successful must be immoral. But that is nothing more than a projection of someone's level of consciousness and their preconceived notions which are a result of programming or self-validation. The success of their realities is a result of frequency alone.

You don't have to like it but you'd be wise to accept it, or you can keep deluding yourself with the idea that a man-made construct exists to the universe.

The only things that exist to the universe are universal constructs. You can't escape these as you are a walking universe, a microcosm of it, a reflection of it. You are bound by the laws of the universe because they are within you.

The nature of the universe is esoterically depicted in the Bible in two verses:

"That ye may be the children of your Father which is in heaven: for he maketh his sun to rise on the evil and on the good, and sendeth rain on the just and on the unjust."

Matthew 5:45

Whether the evil or the good, the just or the unjust, the rain doesn't discriminate. This can be seen across the universe, its laws, and energies.

Rain doesn't target certain people; it doesn't do a criminal background or a credit check, and it definitely doesn't measure your "good deeds."

> *"Then Peter opened his mouth and said: 'In truth I*
> *perceive that God shows no partiality.'"*

Acts 10:34

The esoteric nature of this verse is revealed when you conceptualise God as consciousness, which is the substance of reality.

Consciousness not showing partiality makes it impartial, once again referring to the idea that all treatment is equal and the impersonal nature of consciousness, which simply reflects itself into reality.

Entering your desired reality isn't about becoming a righteous person; it's about becoming the right person to the universe and that's it.

Your morals do not dictate whether you "deserve" your desired reality, your frequency does.

Have you matched the energy of your desired reality? That is all that matters.

You will forever remain in the quicksand of suffering, struggle, misfortune and misery if you moralise the universe. You're communicating in a language it doesn't speak, but that's not even the worst part...

Our notion of "good" and "bad" is nothing more than adhering to the illusion of polarity. It is a confession of our ignorance that everything is one, everyone is one and there is no separation. This dooms us to the reality in which we trap ourselves.

The universe doesn't recognise good or bad because the concept of separation only exists to us.

Even on a humanistic level, good or bad is subjective, but the operation of the universe is totally objective.

We normally moralise the universe in a state of frustration, irritation, apathy, or anger. We call out the heavens:

Why don't we have what we deserve?

Why, despite being good people, are we still suffering?

What did we do to deserve this reality?

This emits a frequency which the universe simply magnifies, plunging us deeper into the very state we hate so much.

This is why those who believe they deserve better will die believing so. Their reality will not change until they realise they're playing the wrong game.

You can't plead your case with the universe on why you deserve a different reality; you must become different; you must emit a different frequency.

This universal truth is somewhat disillusioning, but please don't become apathetic or use it as an excuse to be an impolite, unkind, and unpleasant person.

Do not forget that every individual you meet is simply the same consciousness with a different physical expression; they are you, just with another mask that God is wearing. The way you treat, think, and feel about people is ultimately what you are inviting unto yourself from a point of frequency.

That doesn't mean if you do X to someone, X will be done to you; it means a frequency resonant of X will be with you because you've done it to yourself.

Assuming you're a "good" person, uphold your morals, be polite and be kind. Just make sure that the frequency you're putting out to the universe aligns with your desired reality. That's all the universe cares about.

This is a wakeup call: stop thinking like a human, and start thinking like the universe.

THE FIRST STEP TO MASTERING REALITY

PRINCIPLE

How can you control reality if you can't even control yourself?

How can you expect reality to submit to you if you can't even submit to yourself?

How can you expect reality to listen to your commands if you can't even listen to your commands?

There is no way around it. The first step to controlling your reality is through controlling yourself.

Through self-mastery, what you truly master is reality, and that is because you and reality are one; it is the same entity simply existing on different levels.

The most unused word in the manifestation space is discipline. There is no manifestation without self-mastery.

There is no manifestation without self-discipline.

Nothing is compartmentalised in the mind, and as a result nothing is hidden to the universe. More often than not, what is reflected in the universe is weakness within.

Most people that struggle to manifest don't have difficulty with anything other than mastering themselves, and as a result struggle to master reality.

Truthfully, you do not have a discipline problem.

In fact, nobody has a discipline problem. The true problem is that you are disciplined by the old frequency and not the new one.

You're disciplined in how you see the world.

You're disciplined in how you see people.

You're disciplined in how you label reality.

You're disciplined in how you react to reality.

You're disciplined in how you think.

You're disciplined in how you feel.

You're disciplined in how you focus on certain things.

To live a life that you don't like requires discipline to maintain the frequency of that life. In the same way, to live a life that you do like requires discipline to maintain the frequency of that life.

Discipline isn't an issue, but the irony is there are no truths in reality other than what the subconscious mind accepts as true. When you decide you have no discipline, that is what materialises in your reality.

Recognise how disciplined you have been in order to maintain the old frequency so consistently, and you'll truly realise how powerful you are.

Ironically, the old frequency likes to project the idea that you are weak and lack discipline, so you emit the frequency of weakness as you attempt to materialise your desired reality while hiding the power and strength you have to have to maintain it.

You're more disciplined than you think, and it's your failure to realise this that results in your failed attempts to discipline the new frequency into reality.

Until you recognise the power of that discipline, you will not be able to redirect it towards where you truly want to go.

It seems as though spirituality has become some sort of escapism for those who wish to be liberated from responsibility and discipline; but understand, you will never create your desired reality without them.

Laziness will be tolerated by your old frequency, but not your new frequency.

Self-mastery is the only path to your new frequency, and there is no self-mastery without self-discipline, which means there is no manifestation without self-discipline.

All self-mastery can be summarised with one line:

The ability to follow through on your own conscious commands.

To simplify, it's following through on your own word and establishing your word as law.

There are many spiritual paths and different schools of thought that pursue self-mastery differently, but at their core, they can be boiled down to following through on your conscious direction.

How can you expect to command the universe if you can't even command yourself?

Through commanding yourself, you command the universe.

Commanding ourselves at times can feel like a battle, and in way it is because the old frequency has taken hold of the ego and merged with it to a point where they are indistinguishable.

In the esoteric, the ego isn't a negative trait as society might define it; rather, it's simply the aspect of you that is confined to the physical plane, rooted in the five senses: sight, hearing, taste, touch, and smell.

The ego is nothing more than a vehicle.

I want to make it clear: the ego is not the enemy; unless you perceive it to be so, which then sets in motion you experiencing it as so.

It is the physical expression of the God consciousness.

The ego is a vehicle used to get you from one reality to another.

You are not your body; instead, you animate this avatar, which is the ego.

The ego has been given many names across cultures:

To the religious: the devil.

To Buddhists: the monkey mind.

To spiritualists: the lower self.

To scientists: the primal brain.

The name is irrelevant. Master it or it will master you, and remember, if it does, due to it merging with the old frequency, what will truly master you is the old frequency.

Mastery of reality begins with mastery of the self, and that begins with controlling the ego.

It's the ability to impose your will over the default mode of operation.

You have a way of seeing the world.

You have a way of seeing people.

You have a way of labelling reality.

You have a way of reacting to reality.

You have a way of thinking.

You have a way of feeling.

You have a way of focusing on certain things.

All of the above is your default mode of operation, which can only result in the default frequency being emitted, which can only result in the default reality.

As mentioned earlier, the basis of self-mastery is your ability to follow through on your own conscious direction and commands.

PRACTICAL

Establish your word as law.

There can be no "ifs," "buts," or "maybes;" your command in your life is your final say.

The moment something arises that must be done, you have no choice but to get it done because whether you realise this or not, like this or not, the mind is forever keeping score.

The mind keeps track of all the instances where you say you'll do something and then you don't do it, then it notes that down as "ITFT" for "inability to follow through."

The more ITFTs you get, the less your mind trusts you, which means the less the universe trusts you, which decreases the materialisation of your desired reality.

Conversely, the mind also keeps track of all the instances where you say you'll do something and then you do it, then it notes that down as "ATFT" for "ability to follow through."

The more ATFTs you get, the more your mind trusts you, which means the more the universe trusts you, which increases the materialisation of your desired reality.

If your own mind is against you, then it will feel like the world is against you because your mind and the world are one, so it's best you get your mind on your side.

A harmonious mind is the only blueprint to a harmonious reality.

If you say, "I will wake up at 7 AM," you must do so.

If you decide to complete a task, you must do so.

Whatever the task, establish your word as law. Being your own dictator is the only way you will have the ability to dictate your reality.

It's never about the task itself. The truth is it doesn't matter; all that matters is the significance of you consciously directing yourself.

The issue is that we often establish the word of others as law instead of our own word, which positions them to indirectly dictate the laws of our life.

Here are some examples of when you prioritise the word of others over your own:

- At work, you do as you're told.
- In your family, you do as you're told.
- When someone needs something, you do it.
- When someone needs you to show up for something, you show up.

At what point will you do as you're told, but by *you*?

At what point will you do something when *you* need it to be done?

At what point will you show up for yourself when *you* need to?

When you keep putting off things in your life, without realising it, you are actually putting off self-mastery, which indirectly results in putting off your new frequency.

List all the things you've been putting off and begin to change now. There's no more to it than that.

It is quite literally that simple. Understand that the complications or complexity that is stopping you from seeing that is coming from the old frequency which wants to stay.

Self-mastery is a mandatory, unavoidable, non-negotiable prerequisite to mastery over reality. How could you ever expect to master your reality when you have not mastered yourself?

You cannot, and to think so is to be ignorant of the nature of the universe.

Many are undisciplined yet attempt to discipline the universe. They struggle, never realising their lack of discipline is reflected into the universe.

There is no separation between your mind and the universe. The way you govern yourself is how the universe will govern you, and so long as you are a slave to yourself you will be a slave to reality.

You need to transcend the lower parts of yourself to live in the heights of your dreams.

You may have God within you, but that doesn't qualify you; you must cultivate the God within you by cultivating self-mastery.

You will never control your reality until you can control yourself.

Below I have outlined my personal journey towards self-mastery.

Meditation

Meditation is the cornerstone of spiritual self-mastery.

It involves withdrawing attention from the outer world and turning it inward. The ego is addicted to constant stimulation: notifications, noises, or movement.

The ego will rebel during meditation. You might feel the urge to twitch, scratch, or open your eyes. This resistance is the ego craving stimulation.

By practicing stillness, with your eyes closed, for just 20 minutes daily, you begin to assert dominance over the ego.

It is through stillness that you enter the inner dimension, also known as the "Temple of God," and begin to connect to the infinite, which allows you to extract from the infinite.

"Be still and know that I am God."

Psalm 46:10

When the ego whispers excuses like, "Something's wrong; just open your eyes," resist. This practice builds the very discipline that you will use to alter your reality.

Intermittent Fasting

Intermittent fasting is another effective tool.

Fasting denies the ego a fundamental desire: food.

By fasting, you teach the ego patience and exercise basic control.

When your ego demands satisfaction, respond with, "Not yet." It has no choice but to comply.

Each act of control primes the ego to take commands from you, making future challenges easier to conquer. Over time, you'll find it hard to return to old habits because the benefits of mastery become undeniable.

Be safe and seek medical advice if necessary.

Silence

The practice of silence is transformative.

Silence suppresses the ego's desire to be heard, a primal need embedded in us from infancy.

Babies cry for attention, and as adults, we still crave that validation and expression. Practising silence halts this craving.

Monks often incorporate silence into their discipline because it strips the ego of its need for attention.

It's a powerful form of ego deprivation. Start small: set aside short periods during your day to remain silent, even if you live with others. Just tell them: "I'm mastering reality."

Not everybody's pathway to self-mastery will be the same, so it must be your own.

- Yours could be going to the gym.
- Yours could be replying to messages on time.
- Yours could be not being late anymore.
- Yours could be sticking to your diet.
- Yours could be not drinking or only having one drink.
- Yours could be not shouting.

At a base level, it consists of simply doing what you know you should do, and not doing what you know you shouldn't be doing.

Self-mastery isn't only compartmentalised into "spiritual" practices. The deeper esoteric truth is that everything in reality is spiritual, meaning practice in any aspect is self-mastery. It is your inability to see that which limits the self-mastery you're able to extract.

Your pathway to self-mastery can only be found in your life, by following through on the things you wish to do or change and executing them swiftly.

There's one question lurking in the depths of your mind that is stagnating the energy of your new frequency, blocking it from fully arriving, and it will silently eat away at you until you begin.

Are you the individual that deserves the reality you desire?

Until you can answer that question with a "yes," reality will keep saying "no."

SACRIFICE OR PAY THE UNIVERSE INTEREST

PRINCIPLE

The compound interest of the universe will either be your greatest ally or your worst enemy's worst enemy.

The most dangerous thing in the universe is to not know how it works. Unfortunately, most people live their lives never understanding that their frequency is being multiplied.

Now, one of the most critical fundamentals is what I call the universal compound.

Take the concept of compound interest.

Compound interest just means you get money on your money, and then you get money on that money too, and it just keeps going.

Albert Einstein, who called it the eighth wonder of the world, said: "He who understands it, earns it. He who doesn't, pays it."

Like a snowball rolling downhill, it gets bigger and bigger.

Universal compound is the same thing, just with frequency. The more a frequency multiplies, the more solid it becomes, which solidifies it into reality.

With an understanding of that phenomenon on a universal level, you have the opportunity to earn your desired reality or pay the price.

The longer one is in a particular frequency, the more opportunity that frequency will have to materialise into reality as a condition, circumstance, or event.

After materialising into reality, it now has the opportunity to be an emotionally-intense experience. Since emotion is the language of the subconscious mind, it will reinforce itself deeper and deeper into the subconscious mind.

The longer you're in a frequency, the more it materialises and solidifies its existence into your mind. This can be extrapolated to any experience in reality, whether financial, romantic, health- or career-related.

A simple snowball that gains momentum eventually becomes an avalanche, and it's the same with your frequency.

The unfortunate part about life is that people experience adversity due to nothing more than the universal pendulum swinging back and forth, but then make what should have been only a momentary experience into their reality.

Emotion is the breeding ground for the universal compound effect to take place.

When the energy of emotion gains momentum, it multiples and strengthens, eventually becoming reality.

Momentum is just consistency, and consistency is a form of alchemy.

Consistency is what takes a single vibration and gives it enough momentum to become a rhythm, which becomes a frequency that then becomes a reality.

You can either build positive energetic momentum or negative energetic momentum.

Regardless of who you are or whether it is negative or positive, the universe will multiply that frequency. It will just do what it does.

This is what Christ meant in **Matthew 13:12:**

"Whoever has will be given more, and they will have an abundance. Whoever does not have, even what they have will be taken from them."

The esoteric nature of this verse is all about your energetic momentum.

The frequency that you have will be multiplied, whether that works for or against you. The universe is impersonal in its operation.

This could offer metaphysical insight into why the rich get richer, while the poor get poorer.

The universal compound reveals an unfortunate truth, which is that those who tend to suffer spend the rest of their lives trapped in that suffering because of the universe compounding their frequency.

A snowball that gains momentum has the potential to cause an avalanche.

A small wind that gains momentum has the potential to become a tornado.

The old frequency that you wish to detach from has compounded, and as a result has been expressed through the conditions, circumstances, events, and people in your life.

The old frequency has been able to extract plenty of emotion out of you, and so long as it continues to do so it will multiply itself.

Until you sacrifice the old frequency, there will not be enough space for the new one.

Throughout all civilisations from the beginning of time, it has been understood that to receive something from God or the universe, a sacrifice must be made.

In ancient Egypt (Khemet) and Mesopotamia, people made offerings of food, animals, or valuables to deities to gain favour, protection, or abundance. Temples were built as grand acts of devotion to secure blessings.

In many religious traditions, fasting is a form of sacrifice to purify oneself and receive divine insight or blessings. For example, in Christianity, Lent involves giving up pleasures as an act of devotion. In Islam, Ramadan is a month of fasting that strengthens spiritual connection.

Even in the 21st century, in a non-religious context, the principle still applies. To achieve success, people often sacrifice comfort, time, and immediate gratification.

The point is clear: sacrifice is an inescapable demand of the universe.

Sacrifice typically has negative connotations and is associated with evil and harm, but it is a fundamental law of the universe that is unavoidable, especially in the context of entering your desired reality.

Sacrifice is simply another way of saying exchange.

The prerequisite to you materialising your desired reality is you sacrificing.

You must play by the rules of the universe to win the game, and a foundational truth is that the universe does not operate by creating something from nothing.

You will never gain something from nothing.

Nothing will never produce something.

For something to be gained, something must be exchanged.

This is fractal throughout nature: from photosynthesis, to the food chain, to the nitrogen cycle, at every point there is an exchange.

This is also fractal within the very fabric of your being: you sacrifice one breath to receive another.

The universe is forever in a rhythmic exchange, and since you are a microcosm of the universe, that means you are in a constant rhythmic exchange.

What you exchange is frequency.

You are in a constant cycle of exchanging frequencies for realities, and realities for frequencies. This is the nature of the universe.

To receive a new reality simply requires you to sacrifice your current reality.

The issue is that, unconsciously, more than likely you don't want to sacrifice your current reality, but not for the reasons you think…

Whether you realise this or not, the most addictive substance in the universe isn't any man-made drug: it's frequency.

This why people stay in the same cycles for a long time despite wanting to break free.

This is why people stay in bad situations for a long time despite knowing better.

This is why change feels uncomfortable even when it's for the better – because the mind craves the familiarity of its current frequency.

It's simply an addiction to frequency.

Everybody on the planet is addicted to one frequency or another, but without recognising this you'll never know why, despite wanting better, getting better feels uncomfortable.

The longer you spend in a frequency, the more opportunity you have to experience an emotionally-intense reality which reinforces that condition deeper into your subconscious, which solidifies into your reality.

Many are not ready to give up their old frequency for the new, which logically doesn't make sense but begins to from a metaphysical, energetic perspective.

For something new, a sacrifice must be made, and that sacrifice is you.

The reality you desire requires a new frequency, and so long as you maintain your old one you maintain the old reality.

You must be willing to give up everything you've been for what you could be.

Sacrifice is giving up something of a lower nature for something of a higher nature.

In the same manner that the caterpillar gives up its identity to transform into a butterfly, so must you be willing to give up your old frequency for the new reality.

This revelation presents an opportunity for self-reflection: are you willing to give up your old frequency for your desired reality? This is something only you can answer. Altering your entire reality is no light-hearted gesture; it is radical.

Giving up the old frequency might mean giving up the people associated with it.

Giving up the old frequency might mean giving up the fun parts of it.

Giving up the old frequency might mean giving up the aspects of it that have brought you comfort.

You can't sit in two chairs at once; it is either the old frequency or the new frequency.

Once you give up everything you know, you will realise that the only reason you knew it was because unconsciously you were holding onto it.

PRACTICAL

As stated, you must sacrifice the old frequency, which is simply a matter of giving up the seven keys that make frequency.

Clinging to the old frequency puts you in energetic cuffs which render you unable to move.

You must be willing to give up your current beliefs of what it is you desire to free yourself from the old frequency and move towards the new frequency.

You must be willing to give up your current conviction of what it is you desire to free yourself from the old frequency and move towards the new frequency.

You must be willing to give up your current perception of what it is you desire to free yourself from the old frequency and move towards the new frequency.

You must be willing to give up your current emotionally-charged thoughts of what it is you desire to free yourself from the old frequency and move towards the new frequency.

You must be willing to give up your current focus on what it is you desire to free yourself from the old frequency and move towards the new frequency.

You must be willing to give up your current reactions to what it is you desire to free yourself from the old frequency and move towards the new frequency.

You must be willing to give up your current expectations of what it is you desire to free yourself from the old frequency and move towards the new frequency.

Decide now that everything that used to be will never be your reality.

This will require you to be aware of the instances in your life when you begin to slip back into the old frequency. This awareness can only come by making the decision to be aware.

The uncomfortable truth is that we purposely dismiss awareness because we don't want to be aware. As said many times, ignorance is bliss; but it is also your imprisoner.

THE MECHANICS OF THE UNIVERSE

PRINCIPLE

The universe does not want you to change, and it's all because of the two Ms.

People rarely break out of their cycles.

Those who grow up in a certain set of circumstances typically spend their lives in similar or literally the same circumstances, whether that's financial, romantic, or professional.

At times, it can feel like there is a greater force at play. No matter how much we try to change, it just feels like something wants us to stay the same.

That something is the universe.

As stated at the beginning of this chapter, the universe does not want you to change, and there's a couple reasons for this:

- The universe is a system and, like all systems, it functions best with predictability and minimal deviation.
- It is efficient, favouring whatever is most convenient and requires the least effort.
- By default, it follows the path of least resistance, always seeking to maintain the current state with minimal change.
- As already mentioned, the universe strives for energetic equilibrium, a state of balance. Once something is calibrated to a certain frequency, it will naturally work to preserve that level.

These reasons form the basis of the two Ms of the universe.

The first M is magnify.

Whatever frequency you put out to the universe, it will seek to magnify by using people, conditions, events, and circumstances.

Understand that there is nothing more addictive in this universe than frequency.

Frequency transcends any drug that we humans are capable of making; it is the most addictive substance in the universe.

The universe itself is addicted to whatever is sustaining it, and it will get as much juice from the squeeze as possible at any cost, even to your detriment.

Remember, the largest shareholder of your frequency is emotion, so the universe will magnify your most common emotional state.

If you are in a state of anger, the universe will use people, conditions, events, and circumstances to make you angrier.

If you are in a state of stress, the universe will use people, conditions, events, and circumstances to make you more stressed.

If you are in a state of worry, the universe will use people, conditions, events, and circumstances to make you more worried.

If you are in a state of shame, the universe will use people, conditions, events, and circumstances to make you more ashamed.

If you are in a state of scarcity, the universe will use people, conditions, events, and circumstances to make you have less.

If you are in a state of guilt, the universe will use people, conditions, events, and circumstances to make you more guilty.

If you are in a state of fear, the universe will use people, conditions, events, and circumstances to make you more fearful.

And of course, vice versa.

If you are in a state of joy, the universe will use people, conditions, events, and circumstances to make you more joyful.

If you are in a state of calm, the universe will use people, conditions, events, and circumstances to make you calmer.

If you are in a state of happiness, the universe will use people, conditions, events, and circumstances to make you happier.

If you are in a state of gratitude, the universe will use people, conditions, events, and circumstances to make you more grateful.

If you are in a state of love, the universe will use people, conditions, events, and circumstances to make you more loving.

If you are in a state of abundance, the universe will use people, conditions, events, and circumstances to make you have more.

If you are in a state of security, the universe will use people, conditions, events, and circumstances to make you more secure.

It is addicted to your emotion.

As a result, it will purposely sway your reality, whether negatively or positively, which is solely dependent on your output.

It seeks to get its fix through you.

Remind yourself constantly that the universe is reacting to your frequency. You are not a victim of life; life is a victim of you and the frequency you give it.

The universe is a frequency addict.

The second M of the universe is maintaining.

To revert to energetic equilibrium, the universe likes balance. It also likes efficiency and predictability. To ensure all of that, it will seek to maintain your frequency.

It will do everything in its power to keep you calibrated at your existing level just to make its own life easier.

If you are in a state of anger, the universe will use people, conditions, events and circumstances to keep you in a state of anger.

If you are in a state of stress, the universe will use people, conditions, events and circumstances to keep you in a state of stress.

If you are in a state of worry, the universe will use people, conditions, events and circumstances to keep you in a state of worry.

If you are in a state of shame, the universe will use people, conditions, events and circumstances to keep you in a state of shame.

If you are in a state of scarcity, the universe will use people, conditions, events and circumstances to keep you in a state of scarcity.

If you are in a state of guilt, the universe will use people, conditions, events and circumstances to keep you in a state of guilt.

If you are in a state of fear, the universe will use people, conditions, events and circumstances to keep you in a state of fear.

And of course, vice versa.

If you are in a state of joy, the universe will use people, conditions, events and circumstances to keep you in a state of joy.

If you are in a state of calm, the universe will use people, conditions, events and circumstances to keep you in a state of calm.

If you are in a state of happiness, the universe will use people, conditions, events and circumstances to keep you in a state of happiness.

If you are in a state of gratitude, the universe will use people, conditions, events and circumstances to keep you in a state of gratitude.

If you are in a state of love, the universe will use people, conditions, events and circumstances to keep you in a state of love.

If you are in a state of abundance, the universe will use people, conditions, events and circumstances to keep you in a state of abundance.

If you are in a state of security, the universe will use people, conditions, events and circumstances to keep you in a state of security.

The nature of the universe seeking to maintain our frequency is esoterically explained in **Matthew 13:12**.

"For whoever has, to him more will be given, and he will have abundance; but whoever does not have, even what he has will be taken away from him."

This would metaphysically explain why the rich get richer, and the poor get poorer.

Everything that takes place externally is in the realm of effect, which would include the things normally attributed to the wealthy, such as financial literacy and monopolisation of assets and opportunities.

For those who are rich, the universe will seek to magnify and then maintain their riches; simultaneously, for those who are poor, the universe will seek to magnify and maintain their poverty.

These two mechanisms of the universe can be indeed frustrating. Why does it seem so difficult to switch frequencies and switch realities?

Don't make the mistake of thinking switching realities is difficult, because believing it will make it so.

It will require some initial effort before momentum is built.

The longer you spend in your new frequency, the more it compounds, the stronger it gets and so the more addicted the universe becomes to it. Then, it'll seek to magnify and maintain it for you.

Consistency is a form of alchemy.

So, decide that switching realities will be easy and require minimal effort, and you will experience it as so.

Most people live their lives feeling as if they're trapped in the same cycles, unaware of the two Ms.

The universe likes cycles; they're predictable and efficient.

The truth is, you will never be able to break the cycle.

You will always find yourself in a cycle. That is inescapable, and to desire otherwise will only result in frustration and failure.

The alchemist never attempts to go against the nature of the universe but will use the nature of the universe against itself; and so, you must not attempt to break any cycle.

You must switch cycles.

The law of energy conservation states that energy can neither be created nor destroyed; rather, it can only be transformed or transferred from one form to another.

Extrapolate this to the cycles in which we are stuck:

Cycles can neither be created nor destroyed; rather, they can only be transformed or transferred from one form to another.

It's not about creating new cycles or destroying old ones, but simply switching the cycle you're in for another.

PRACTICAL

The first step to freeing yourself from the cycle in which you're trapped is becoming more aware.

Awareness will always be the prerequisite to any form of transformation. In relation to the two Ms, you must become aware of what is first being magnified and eventually maintained.

Before desiring for reality to change, see that you have first changed. It is vain to be dissatisfied with reality but satisfied with yourself.

What is your day-to-day mood?

What is your daily attitude?

What is your base emotional state?

Until you become aware of these things, and clearly define them, you do not possess the necessary faculties to switch from your current cycle (or condition of reality) to another.

Honesty is a must; you can lie to others but you can never lie to the universe. It will show you the truest indication of who you are in the depths of your mind.

Do you feel defeated?

Do you feel irritated?

Do you feel frustrated?

Do you feel hopeless?

Do you feel stressed?

Do you feel worried?

Do you feel inadequate?

Do you feel angry?

Do you feel sad?

Do you feel ashamed?

Do you feel guilty?

Assuming you feel stuck in a cycle of reality you don't like, chances are you are feeling one or more of these.

If you want to manifest something specific, what is your day-to-day mood in reference to it?

Let's say you want to attract a romantic partner:

Do you feel unlovable?

Do you feel ugly?

Do you feel unseen?

Do you feel unappreciated?

Do you feel lonely?

Or, let's say you want a better job:

Do you feel unqualified for that position?

Do you feel undeserving of that position?

Do you feel unseen by your colleagues?

Or, let's say you want more money:

Do you worry about your financial security?

Do you feel like money hates you?

Determine how you feel. If you pinpoint it accurately enough, you will see that very feeling reflected, magnified, and maintained in the universe.

After awareness, the next step is transformation. This is a simple process of changing the way you're feeling on a da-y-to-day basis to its energetic opposite polarity.

Polarity, also known as duality, is simply about separation and the truth that everything within our third-dimensional realm has energetic opposites, for example hot-cold, masculine-feminine, negative-positive.

Everything has its complementary energetic opposite. Remember that you're never stuck with only one option or condition of reality, despite what it would like for you to believe.

The way that you've been consistently feeling has an energetic opposite, which is the same energy just vibrating at a different rate. As long as you can alter your rate of vibration, you can alter your frequency, ultimately altering your reality.

After you've accurately pinpointed your base mood, the next step is altering your vibration.

Altering your vibration is simply a matter of altering your concentration.

Whether you realise this or not, you've been concentrating on aspects of your unwanted reality that reflect the very same feelings you feel trapped by.

This is how the cycle continues.

Think of polarities like living entities.

Both polarities fight for as much energy as possible. When one has received some energy, it'll convince you that the other polarity doesn't exist to siphon as much as it can.

Those who feel like a burden for some reason can't conceptualise that it's possible to feel cherished.

Those who feel stressed for some reason can't conceptualise that it's possible to feel peaceful.

Those who feel rejected for some reason can't conceptualise that it's possible to feel accepted.

Those who feel unwanted for some reason can't conceptualise that it's possible to feel wanted.

The polarity that is focused upon will eventually present itself as the only thing on the menu, hiding the truth that there is another option that can be chosen just as easily.

Awareness of this misdirection of energy is the prerequisite to transmuting and experiencing the energy you wish to see reflected in reality.

Assuming you've come to the conclusion of wanting to get rid of the feeling you've been maintaining, you must now identify its complementary energetic polarity.

If on a daily basis you feel unseen, the complementary energetic polarity would be feeling seen.

If on a daily basis you feel unappreciated, the complementary energetic polarity would be feeling appreciated.

If on a daily basis you feel like a burden, the complementary energetic polarity would be feeling cherished.

If on a daily basis you feel defeated, the complementary energetic polarity would be feeling victorious.

If on a daily basis you feel irritated, the complementary energetic polarity would be feeling patient.

If on a daily basis you feel stressed, the complementary energetic polarity would be feeling relieved.

You get the idea. If your feeling isn't on the list, I'm sure you'll figure it out.

After defining the polarity of the energy you'd wish to experience, the next step is simply focusing on its existence in your life already.

The unwanted polarity that you've been magnifying doesn't just hide the concept of a complementary energetic polarity; it also filters out the moments in your life when you experience the positive polarity.

By doing so, it keeps you unaware of the wanted energy, and so it keeps the wanted energy unaware of you.

The universe defines concentration as a centralisation of energy, either directly, implicitly, resonantly, or reflectively.

Unconsciously, you've been focusing on the experiences and aspects of your life that imply the feeling that is being magnified, leading to the unwanted reality.

Unconsciously, you've been focusing on the experiences and aspects of your life that resonate with the feeling that is being magnified, leading to the unwanted reality.

Unconsciously, you've been focusing on the experiences and aspects of your life that reflect the feeling that is being magnified, leading to the unwanted reality.

It's nothing to do with your reality; it's everything to do with you.

It is your frequency that distorts reality to reflect your frequency, and this works positively and negatively.

When we experience "reality," we aren't really experiencing reality but ourselves, because you cannot see anything in reality that is not of you.

Reality just *is*. It's neutral, but through the emotional state you hold day-to-day you only focus on the parts that resonate, reflect and imply how you feel.

To shift from one pole to another simply requires you to concentrate on the pole you'd like to experience, excluding the pole you no longer wish to experience.

That means focusing on the experiences and aspects of your life that reflect the energetic polarity you wish to experience.

That means focusing on the experiences and aspects of your life that imply the energetic polarity you wish to experience.

That means focusing on the experiences and aspects of your life that resonate with the energetic polarity you wish to experience.

Instead of allowing the world to affirm how you feel, allow how you feel to affirm the world.

To reiterate, pick the polarity that you'd like to see magnified in your reality and focus on the experiences and aspects of your life that confirm its existence.

Whether these are significant events or not, it doesn't really matter as there is no big or small to the infinite – there is only frequency to be compounded.

I'll give a couple of examples to help you better conceptualise the process.

In the case of wanting to attract a romantic partner:

Do you feel unlovable? The complementary energetic polarity is being lovable -> Focus on the experiences and aspects of your life when people have shown you love, big or small -> Immerse yourself in the feeling of that love and realise that you're lovable.

Do you feel unappreciated? The complementary energetic polarity is being appreciated -> Focus on the experiences and aspects of your life when people have shown you appreciation, big or small -> Immerse yourself in the feeling of that appreciation and realise that you're appreciated.

In the case of wanting a better job:

Do you feel unqualified? The complementary energetic polarity is being qualified -> Focus on the experiences and aspects of your life when you have been qualified, big or small -> Immerse yourself in the feeling of being qualified and realise that you're qualified.

Do you feel undeserving? The complementary energetic polarity is being deserving -> Focus on the experiences and aspects of your life when people have shown that you are deserving, big or small -

> Immerse yourself in the feeling of being deserving and realise that you deserve it.

In the case of attracting more money:

Do you feel that money doesn't come easily to you? The complementary energetic polarity is money does come easily to you-> Focus on the experiences and aspects of your life when money did come easily to you, big or small -> Immerse yourself in the feeling of money coming easily to you and realise it does.

This is a skill. The more you do it, the easier it'll become, but just decide at the start it'll be easy and let your mind do the rest.

THE ANNOYING LAW OF THE UNIVERSE

PRINCIPLE

You can only have what you already have, and if you don't already have it, you can never have it.

At first glance, the statement above seems paradoxical, but it is only paradoxical so long as you don't understand the annoying law of the universe.

Until you understand the annoying law of the universe, reality will continue to be annoying. Especially in the context of creating your desired reality, this law cannot be avoided. It bears repeating:

You can only have what you already have.

If you don't have your desired reality, then you'll never have it.

Yes, you read that right. You need to have your desired reality in order to have it.

There's two chairs in the universe, and you can't sit in both of them simultaneously. You're either in one or the other, and only one will sit you in your desired reality.

The first chair of the universe is wanting.

You will never manifest anything you want. You can't have anything you want.

Before we go deeper into this, I want to make something crystal clear: manifesting your desired reality isn't about what *you* understand or think. It's about what the *universe* understands and thinks, so we must adhere to its psyche. Within the psyche of the universe, wanting is an indication that you do not have your desired reality because you only want something that you don't have.

Think about it: do you want your current reality? No, because you already have it.

But it gets a bit more intricate once we discover the unobvious connotations that the universe associates with wanting, and that is importance.

The universe interprets wanting as importance. It also interprets importance as energetic space: the bigger the importance, the bigger the space in between you and your desired reality.

Think about it like this:

The people that need money the most have the least.

The people that need money the least have the most.

An unfortunate reality that should be otherwise, but don't attempt to moralise the universe; it doesn't adhere to what should be, it only adheres to what is.

To simplify, and reiterate, you can't have any reality that you want because to want is to confess that you do not have, and if you don't already have it, you can't have it.

The second chair of the universe is having.

This is the only way you'll enter your desired reality.

Reality will only give you whatever you already have, but not by your definition of having but the universe's definition.

The human definition of having pertains to the physical plane, which is playing the game backwards.

Your definition of having is probably being able to see or touch your desired reality. So long as you're adhering to this definition that the universe doesn't recognise, you're speaking a language that the universe doesn't.

The universe doesn't take reality to be real because reality is an illusion, so "having" anything in the third dimensional doesn't mean anything to the universe.

You need to have, not by the human definition which is tied to an illusion, but by the universe's definition which is tied to frequency.

The universe's definition of having is your frequency or state of consciousness; that is more real than anything in reality.

It is the mental and emotional declaration of who you are now.

Think about it like this: the universe registers you by whatever frequency you put out to it. It sees your frequency as the totality of your beliefs, conviction, perception, emotionally-charged thoughts, focus, reactions, and expectations.

To have your desired reality by the universe's definition, each one of those attributes needs to reflect your desired reality.

It's not a game of manifesting; it's a game of vibrationally aligning with your desired reality.

The less you want your desired reality, the easier it'll come because the universe won't register any energetic space between you and it.

How effortlessly do unwanted outcomes manifest in your life?

The more you want your desired reality, the harder it'll come because the universe will register energetic space between you and it, keeping you separate from it.

How much resistance do you experience when trying to manifest what you desire?

It seems as though our desires work against us, and it's because our desires are a confession that we don't have them.

Those who desire approval lack the state they believe approval would put them in.

Those who desire respect lack the state they believe respect would put them in.

Those who desire money lack the state they believe money would put them in.

Those who desire love lack the state they believe love would put them in.

Have you given yourself your desired reality? (Not by your definition, but the universe's).

An unfortunate truth of reality is that nothing is lacking from us except that which we fail to give ourselves. God or the universe aren't holding anything back.

The only way to truly have your desired reality is to give it to yourself.

Desires are what you seek externally, but to seek outside of yourself is to stare into the abyss of an illusion that does not exist. If you stare unknowingly into what does not exist, how could you ever expect your desired realities to exist?

What you have is what you seek for internally, and to seek inside of yourself is to stare into the truth. When you recognise this, you no longer chase illusions but embody the reality you wish to experience. By knowing that what you seek is already present, you allow your desired realities to manifest effortlessly.

Anything and everything you desire externally is simply what you are missing internally.

Giving yourself the reality you desire is simply a process of internally, intensely, and vividly experiencing what you desire within instead of without.

When done with intensity, an internal shift will occur that diminishes the very desire that is repelling what you desire away from you.

While this law is annoying, it's also liberating when you come to one realisation...

You possess everything you'll ever need to reach any frequency or state of consciousness, which means any desired reality. Only through first acquiring the frequency or state of consciousness will you enter your desired reality.

If you're not already in your desired reality then you can never be in your desired reality.

If it is more money you desire, you must already have it to have it.

If it is a new career you desire, you must already have it to have it.

If it is a loving and healthy relationship you desire, you must already have it to have it.

The moment you "have" by the universe's definition, you will "have" by the human definition.

Before you can be in your dream reality, you must be in your dream reality in your current reality. Until you can treat your current life like it's your dream life, it can never be.

The good thing about this law is that it can give you true insight into your current state of consciousness, which makes you aware of the reality you're creating.

Pinpointing whether you already have what you desire only requires answering the following questions:

Are you good with your desired reality?

Are you good without your desired reality?

Could you live happily if your desired reality never manifested?

Would your desired reality manifesting make you happier than you are now?

Would your desired reality manifesting give you more inner peace than you have now?

Would your desired reality manifesting make you feel more whole and complete than you are now?

Every once in a while, as you're doing the inner work and rearrangements, come back to those questions to gauge your progress. Don't bother lying; you can lie to yourself but never to the universe. It has the ultimate lie detector: a frequency detector.

The more your frequency aligns with your desired reality, the less you'll need your desired reality, and that's when it'll need you.

The annoying law of the universe is truly embodied by its complementary frequency, which is the secret frequency of not needing, and you will have touched it at some point in your life.

The secret frequency of not needing is what will make your desired reality chase you. It simply has one rule, and one rule only:

You can't have what you need, but you can have anything you don't need.

There have been instances in your life that you have almost effortlessly been able to materialise things that you did not want.

The strange thing about reality is that what we don't want or care about often comes to us effortlessly, while the things we deeply want or care for seem to resist us the most.

The truths of the universe are hidden in clichés:

- You finally stop looking for your keys and then they appear in plain sight.
- You spend hours trying to remember a name, give up, and suddenly it pops into your head.
- You apply to dozens of jobs and hear nothing... then a company you weren't even chasing reaches out.
- You desperately want to impress someone, yet they're not interested. But when you're just being yourself with no agenda, people are drawn to you.
- You chase after clients, opportunities or sales and hit a wall... then land a major deal out of the blue when you're relaxed and detached.
- You try to force creativity and nothing comes. The moment you take a break for shower, the idea downloads effortlessly.
- You want to sleep so badly that you can't, but the moment you stop trying, you drift off.

The harder you try, the less the universe complies.

The issue is this: when your desired reality feels like it can do more for you than you can do for yourself, you're unknowingly signalling to the universe that you've forgotten who you truly are. Reality only bows to the one who knows themselves.

When you're anchored in your true identity, which is a materialisation of God, you realise the world has nothing to offer you that you don't already possess within. From that place, *you* become the source, not the seeker.

Too many are seekers, and too few are sources.

Before you desire anything in reality, first become a source of it.

If you seek money, be a source of it by tipping, donating, or giving freely.

If you seek love, be a source of it by showing affection to those already in your life.

If you seek appreciation, be a source of it by letting those around you know that you are grateful they are in your life.

There are things in your life that you can materialise easily, and even unwillingly. This is simply you unconsciously using the secret frequency of not needing.

Often, the things that come to you easily are precisely those things you never actively sought or even wanted.

The individual who seems to attract multiple partners more than likely isn't seeking them or wanting them.

The individual who seems to attract a multitude of opportunities more than likely isn't seeking them or wanting them.

The individual who always impresses those around them more than likely isn't seeking to impress them.

This power might seem mystical or even magical, but it's not; it's something you've been using your entire life. Like most things, the shift isn't about discovering something new but about moving from unconscious use to conscious mastery.

There are things that come naturally to you: skills, talents or manifestations that flow with ease for you but with which others struggle.

You may not even recognise them as special because they feel effortless to you. But that effortlessness is the power.

Don't let your desire for what you don't have blind you to the areas where you're already powerful. Whether it's communication, creativity, dancing, making money, attracting opportunities, solving problems or making people laugh, there's something you do with ease that others admire or wish they could replicate.

Only you know what that is, and don't be so foolish to think there's nothing.

If you think there's nothing, that's just your old frequency keeping your power hidden from you.

The irony is you probably see your magic as nothing special.

Chances are you dismiss as insignificant or overlook entirely those things you already manifest effortlessly through the secret frequency of not needing. But that effortless flow, the thing you barely think twice about, is the source of your magic.

What feels like "nothing" to you is the very source of power.

PRACTICAL

When you desire nothing, the world will seek to give you everything.

Biblically, Yeshua was approached by the devil in the desert, who offered him all the kingdoms of the world, everything he could see, if he would simply bow down in submission. But the only reason such an offer was made is because Yeshua was unmoved by everything.

There was nothing the world could give him, because once you realise your true identity as part of the infinite, the material becomes insignificant. When you know who you are, the world has nothing to offer, and that's precisely when it tries to offer you everything.

The things that do nothing for you will seek to do everything for you.

However, the things that do everything for you will end up doing nothing for you.

To the universe, obsession is repulsion.

To the universe, desperation is disrespect.

The moment you detach from your desire, it'll do everything to attach itself to you.

Activating the secret frequency of not needing simply requires you to look at your desired reality in the same way you look at the things you don't want that you easily materialise.

Look at your desired reality as unimportant.

Look at your desired reality as insignificant.

Look at your desired reality as if it is nothing.

Through minimising your perception towards your desired reality, you neutralise it. You normalise it in your subconscious mind, making it normal in your reality.

You have given yourself so many things that you already effortlessly materialise that you are almost tired of them, unmoved by them; that same energy must be applied to your desired reality.

Luckily, the more you use the technique prescribed for manifestation, the more you naturally set it into motion, since you are giving yourself what the world hopes to give you.

"ON EARTH, AS IT IS IN HEAVEN"

PRINCIPLE

No heaven, no manifestation.

You will not materialise your desired reality until you live in heaven.

There are prerequisites to materialising your desired reality, and one of them is entering heaven; not in the religious sense of a particular location in the afterlife, but in the metaphysical sense.

Most people make the mistake of attempting to materialise their desired reality without realising that the frequency in which they live and exist is in direct opposition to what they want.

It's safe to say that most of the world live in hell, and you can only ever be where you are.

In the religious sense, hell and heaven are locations in the afterlife that one enters depending upon how they lived their life in accordance to the will of their God. But these two locations exist on Earth, specifically within your consciousness.

> *"Nor will they say, 'See here!' or 'See there!' For indeed, the kingdom of God is within you."*

Luke 17:21

Christ stated very plainly that the kingdom of God, which is synonymous with heaven, isn't outside of you or in the sky, but within you.

This idea directly contradicts the notion of heaven being location in the afterlife as religious institutions have been marketing to the masses for thousands of years.

For more context, Christ was talking to his people and explaining how others will point you to a place and say that the kingdom of God is here or there, but you should not fall for it because "the kingdom of God is within you."

The idea of heaven being within you should lead to an internal restructuring and redefining of what heaven is.

How can you go to a place that is within you?

Why would I have to die to go to a place that is within me?

How is it that when you die you will go to heaven but Christ says it is within you?

To reaffirm **Luke 17:21**, in the lost Gospel of Thomas, Christ explains the same concept.

> *"Jesus said, 'If those who lead you say to you, "See, the kingdom is in the sky," then the birds of the sky are closer than you. If they say to you, "It is in the sea," then the fish already know it. Rather, the kingdom is inside of you, and it is outside of you."'*

The truth is, until heaven is metaphysically defined, your desired reality will be confined.

Heaven isn't a location in the afterlife; it is the immersion into the formless state of absolute awareness, a unification with the infinite intelligence, also known as God.

In this unification with God, the mind is unburdened by attachment, resistance, temporal limitation, desire, wants or needs, and it requires nothing for it has everything.

Heaven isn't a place but a realisation: the direct knowing of self as the infinite, unfragmented whole. In this state, separation from God dissolves, suffering ceases and experience aligns with effortless inner calm, peace and bliss.

The irony is, whether you realise this or not, you have touched heaven at some point in your life.

That inner stillness, peace, calm where you were in complete fulfilment and felt whole, desiring nothing because you felt connected to everything.

Heaven is not a place you get to, but a place you realise is already here within you.

It is the silent backdrop behind all illusion, accessible the moment one surrenders the need to seek the world for what only it can give you.

Hell, being the energetic polarity of heaven, is also not a particular location in the afterlife; like heaven, it is a state of consciousness, a frequency in which many do not realise they are already living.

Hell is immersion into the physical plane, a lack of awareness for the other planes of existence leading one to be consumed by the ego, which takes the world around to be the only truth, also known as the devil.

This unification with the devil (the ego), a consciousness burdened by attachment, resistance, temporal limitation, desire, wants and needs, requires everything due to a distortion in perception where one fails to realise one has everything.

Hell isn't a place but a failure to realise and see oneself as the infinite, unfragmented whole. Hell is often described as a separation from God, but since God is omnipresent, that doesn't make sense. Hell is misalignment from God.

This misalignment leads to suffering, inner chaos, conflict, and restlessness, despite the illusion that material possessions can resolve those things.

The irony is, whether you realise this or not, you have touched hell at some point in your life.

That inner chaos and conflict, where you felt a lack of fulfilment or completion leading to a sense of being disconnected.

Nobody can escape the truth that reality is nothing more than immaterialised frequency, and any frequency maintained will be materialised.

Many desire heaven while maintaining a frequency which resonates with hell. Those who live in a hellish state can only experience hell, and those who live in a heavenly state can only experience heaven.

The path to heaven can only be walked by those in heaven. Reality will never precede consciousness; effect will never precede cause.

You can only have what you already have, and if the frequency you're emanating to the universe is hellish, it cannot possibly not bring you to heaven.

Apple seeds will never produce mangoes, and mango seeds will never produce apples. This is a simple truth in the world of nature, and it reflects how the universe works.

In the modern day, hell is equivalent to living in survival mode.

From a neuroscientific point of view, when one is living in survival mode it is typically due to a lack of safety, which triggers the primal brain into operation.

The primal brain has no other purpose than survival; flight or fight and nothing else.

While survival mode is often associated with poverty, paradoxically, wealthy people also live in survival mode.

Since the primal brain is responsible for flight or fight, its only concern is surviving by hyper-focusing on what is immediately in front of it.

This zeroing in on reality restricts our level of awareness, which means a limited perspective.

This reduction in awareness and perspective shuts down higher levels of thinking since survival is the priority.

A lower level of awareness will always lead to reality being distorted to reflect the lower aspects of one's nature, which will always correlate with negativity.

Hell is directly opposed to the materialisation of your desired reality metaphysically. In neuroscientific terms, it is specifically opposed to your brain waves.

The alteration of reality requires an alteration of one's frequency or one's state of consciousness, which requires an alteration of one's subconscious mind.

The subconscious mind becomes more accessible in certain brainwave states, allowing for deeper influence and transformation. By leveraging the optimal brainwave frequencies, you can achieve more with less effort, as your mind becomes more receptive to change.

To revert to the point initially made at the start of this chapter, until you can enter heaven you will not be able to enter your desired reality. This is due to the fact that what we metaphysically consider to be heaven, when it comes to brainwaves, is the door to the subconscious mind.

There are various brainwaves that the brain cycles throughout the day.

- Beta waves (12-30Hz)
- Alpha waves (8-12Hz)
- Theta waves (4-8Hz)
- Delta waves (0.5-4Hz)

Beta waves are associated with being awake, alert and active; it is the standard mode of operation in your day-to-day life.

Alpha waves are associated with a meditative, relaxed state; it is the state before drowsiness.

Theta waves are associated with deep meditation, a trance-like state which is typically used in hypnosis and is equivalent to a drowsy state.

Delta waves are associated with deep sleep.

The slower the brain waves, the closer they are to the subconscious mind.

Beta waves are produced during conscious operation, and so long as the conscious mind is present, the subconscious mind won't be.

Think about these brainwave states like trains: the slower the brainwave state, the easier it is to catch a ride to the subconscious mind.

The slow trains are your only entry into the subconscious mind.

Most people make the mistake of attempting to give the subconscious mind their desired reality to materialise while operating in a brainwave state that prioritises the conscious mind.

To put it another way, they are trying to catch the fast trains, which only lead to the conscious mind and not the subconscious mind.

The brainwaves we produce are interconnected with either heaven or hell.

Those who live in a survival state of consciousness rarely relax. Their alertness means they mainly produce beta waves, which are the fastest waves that call upon the operation of the conscious mind and not the subconscious mind.

Therefore, all attempts to alter their frequency, or state of consciousness or subconscious mind, are made in vain. They're trying to catch a train that doesn't lead to the subconscious mind.

Those who live in a survival state of consciousness live in hell; and those who live in hell produce beta waves, which means they never access their subconscious mind.

Could this be the reason so many of those who live in survival mode struggle to alter their minds?

Alternatively, those who live in a heavenly state of consciousness are always relaxed, mainly producing alpha and theta waves, which are slower and lead to the subconscious rather than conscious mind.

Therefore, all attempts to alter their frequency, or state of consciousness or subconscious mind, are effortless and successful because they're trying to catching a train that leads to the subconscious mind.

It is much easier for a car to drive on smooth, calm roads than roads filled with bumps, and potholes.

In the same manner, it is much easier for a boat to sail on calm waters. The more relaxed you are day to day, the more likely your brain will be producing waves that are conducive to what you're trying to put into your subconscious mind.

The less relaxed you are, the less likely your brain will be producing waves that are conducive to what you're trying to put in your brain.

The truth of brain waves and their interconnection to the two states of consciousness is highlighted esoterically in **John 3:27.**

"John answered and said, 'A man can receive nothing, except it be given him from heaven.'"

Nothing you desire on this physical plane will ever be attained unless you are already in the frequency of being in heaven.

Metaphysically, to live in a heavenly state is to exist with inner calm, peace, bliss, fulfilment and to desire nothing, which would indicate to the universe that you have everything.

It's likely that the attainment of your desired reality would produce the state above, so the state above would produce the attainment of your desired reality.

Attaining your desired reality would bring you peace, inner calm and bliss, so peace, inner calm and bliss can also bring your desired reality.

Relaxation is the prerequisite for brainwaves that allow for easy access to the subconscious mind, which is the womb of reality.

To receive, the prerequisite is to be in a heavenly state; conversely, those in hell never receive.

Another Bible verse encapsulates what I call the heavenly order of manifestation:

"But seek first the kingdom of God and his righteousness, and all these things will be added to you."

Matthew 6:33

Here, the heavenly order of manifestation is established.

Before seeking the materiality of your desired reality – instead of seeing the money, the wealth, the partner, the career or whatever it is you desire – you must first seek a heavenly state of consciousness.

Calm the waters before you set sail.

Here's the issue: part of you believes that once you get your desired reality you'll feel complete, fulfilled, satisfied, calm, and relaxed without realising that if you aren't already those things you cannot have them.

The bigger problem is that if you don't have them currently, then you indicate to the universe that you have their opposites which are emptiness, unfulfillment, dissatisfaction and chaos, which are what will be reflected.

Anytime that you go against the heavenly order of manifestation you unconsciously descend into the hellish order of manifestation, which will only lead to hell.

If you put your desires above heaven, then your desires will always be out of reach.

Until you recognise that where you think you'll be after getting your desired reality is where you need to start from, you'll never arrive.

Seek first to be internally fulfilled, satisfied, calm, and relaxed without your desired reality and all the "things" you want will be given to you because to be in that state indicates to the universe that you already have them.

The universe will never bow before the one who bows before illusion.

The only way to get those "things" you desire is to enter heaven by first giving them to yourself, not in the humanistic way but the universal way.

At this point, it should be clear that relaxation is the prerequisite to revealing your desired reality; that's non-negotiable.

PRACTICAL

Relaxation is your natural state, which I understand seems counterintuitive given the hectic, stressful nature of today's world.

If relaxation is the mandatory step to materialising your desired reality, those who are never relaxed can never truly materialise their desired reality.

True relaxation arises from disconnecting from the outside world, and that is because it is the world that seeks to keep you from relaxation.

It seeks to siphon your peace of mind by getting you to focus on work, your inadequacies, family dramas, politics or the latest war.

How can you relax when the mind is so preoccupied?

I'm not suggesting you neglect the outside world, rather encouraging you to pay attention to your inner world, so when you pay attention to the world it receives what it deserves from you.

Relaxation is when the mind is occupied by nothing; only you can make yourself relaxed.

Anything that can make you relaxed can take that feeling away, and true relaxation is independent to any person, any condition and any circumstance.

Whatever the world gives you, it can take from you – and, at some point, it most definitely will.

To immerse yourself into nothingness, to reach that inner stillness, is the true pathway to relaxation; to seek refuge in the inner world instead of the outer world is how you are granted protection by the heavenly government.

To be still is to do nothing. Whether you meditate or not, make a practice of doing nothing.

Naturally, the mind will begin to tell you how difficult it is to relax, but that is the old frequency speaking. It wants to exist without relaxation as it knows that is the stepping stone to your new frequency.

Difficulty aside, what other choice do you have than to relax?

YOU CAN'T OUTRUN YOUR FREQUENCY

PRINCIPLE

Manifestation cannot occur without a synchronised alignment across all three levels of existence.

Various cultures and traditions across the world adhere to the notion of three levels of existence.

The three planes of existence have many different names:

Mind, body, and spirit.

God the father, God the son, and God the holy spirit.

Mental plane, physical plane, and spiritual plane.

These are simply different expressions of the same universal truth.

The inability to change one's reality often stems from ignorance of the three levels of existence. Most people go through life operating from only one plane while completely neglecting the other two.

But relying on just one aspect of your being is guaranteed to lead to stagnation and a death sentence for your desired reality. True transformation requires full-spectrum alignment: mental, physical, and spiritual planes working as one.

Manifestation is impossible without a synchronised alignment across all three levels of existence. This is the multi-dimensional structure of reality.

The plane of existence that most solely use is the physical.

This is what you call reality.

It's everything you've ever known: everything you can see, touch, taste, smell and hear. It is the realm of your physical vessel, which is the materialisation or the "image" of God.

Despite the physical plane appearing to be real, it is an illusion. This doesn't mean it's fake; it just means there's more to it than meets the eye.

Scientifically speaking, humans can only perceive a tiny fraction of the electromagnetic spectrum, the range known as visible light.

This visible light makes up approximately 0.0035% of the full electromagnetic spectrum, meaning 99.995% of the spectrum is invisible to the human eye.

There is a vast and active part of the universe that we simply can't perceive with our senses.

Reality is like putting on a VR headset and forgetting that you are wearing one.

When you put on a VR headset, you become fully immersed in a simulated world.

You can look around, interact, and even feel emotions based on what you see, even though none of it is physically real. The headset filters your experience, creating a reality that feels true, even though it's just a projection.

Consciousness works the same way. It acts like an internal "headset" that filters how you see the world. You're not experiencing reality as it is; you're experiencing reality through the lens of your consciousness.

What you perceive outside is a reflection of the system running inside.

You're not reacting to the world but how your consciousness is interpreting it – like wearing a VR headset and forgetting that you have it on.

For centuries, ancient mystics have known of this illusion, referring to it as the world of maya.

It is the realm of effect. All you experience here – every circumstance of failure, success, poverty or wealth – is merely the shadow cast by the mind: an effect.

Reality is an effect: smoke from a fire, ripples in a pond, an echo of sound, a reflection from a mirror.

Most of the world operates from this one plane of existence simply because it's all their mind can conceive of existing.

Being tied to the physical plane, they tie themselves down.

To reiterate, the physical plane is the realm of effect. The mistake that you must not make is attempting to change an effect itself. Reality cannot truly be changed from reality; it must be altered on a higher plane of existence.

The only place from where reality can truly be changed is the mental plane.

Where do thoughts come from? Is every thought mine?

Think of the mental plane as a layer of immaterialised thought, like clouds of potential ideas drifting through the fabric of reality.

Imagine the world is made of steam: you can't touch it, but when its vibration is altered it forms matter, which in this example would be ice.

The physical plane is nothing more than the mental plane materialised.

The mental plane is interchangeable with the mind, your state of consciousness, or your frequency.

The mental plane is outside of our third-dimensional realm, meaning it isn't confined by the illusions of space and time; time isn't linear as we experience it in our reality.

This reveals a truth you may not have heard: you don't create reality. How could you? Everything already exists, and it exists here.

Think about it like this: you go to a restaurant and for the meals are already prepared. You simply select which one you want.

This notion is instantly liberating because it removes all the pressure that unconsciously comes with the idea that you need to create. No! Everything has already been created. You just need to choose, which is something to which your mind is more adjusted.

The mental plane exists within the subconscious mind specifically.

Being the realm of cause, it is the fire that produces smoke, the stone that creates ripples, the voice that generates an echo, the light that casts a shadow and the object that reflects in the mirror.

You can only experience physically what first existed mentally; you cannot escape this cause-and-effect chain reaction.

Remember, everything you see in reality was first a thought, a form of imagination, just not yet tangible. This must be extrapolated to every condition, circumstance, and event that you experience in reality.

The spiritual plane is where your spirit body exists. Some call it the astral body, hence terms such as astral projection.

Delving too deeply into the spiritual plane is beyond the scope of this book, so I will keep it directly relevant to reality creation.

Your spirit is the aspect of you that is infinite.

This means it is beyond the illusions of the third-dimensional realm. It is the droplet from the ocean of God, and the thing about a droplet is that it contains the same qualities and properties as the entire ocean.

It is on this plane that your connection to God is determined; not in a religious, please-your-parents sense, but in your ability to unify with the infinite intelligence and harmonise with the energy of God.

The spiritual plane is like the oven that bakes your mental creation into the physical plane. The stronger your connection to God, the quicker you'll be able to materialise conditions into reality and the greater you'll be able to materialise into reality.

To reiterate, this isn't in a religious sense. It's about what your state of being is indicating to the universe.

All three planes of existence must be harmonised in order for your desired reality to be materialised, which would mean:

The mental plane is harmonised with your desired reality.

The physical plane is harmonised with your desired reality.

The spiritual plane is harmonised with your desired reality.

Since there are three levels of existence, there seems to be three modes of operation when it comes to progression in reality:

The physical planers: These are the people that work as long and hard as possible, grinding away day and night.

The mental planers: These are the people that just think about what they want all day without taking any form of action, hoping everything they want will just magically come to them.

The spiritual planers: These are the people that just pray to God about what they want all day without taking any form of action, hoping God will simply give it to them.

The hard worker, the hard thinker, and the hard prayer are all dwelling in the same ignorance but their vanity has them think otherwise.

They are all making the same mistake of simply relying on one plane of existence instead of using all three in unison.

Let's examine the multi-dimensional mistakes they are all making:

The physical planers:

They are unaware that reality is an effect, which they are attempting to also change with an effect.

They rely solely on physical action, neglecting the higher planes of existence and never realising that action is the lowest level of consciousness so their results are low-level.

This is where most of the world reside, without ever realising that you cannot change an effect itself, you must change the cause.

You cannot outrun your frequency.

You cannot outhustle your frequency.

You cannot work your way out of your frequency.

The mental planers:

They are unaware that action is the external manifestation of the internal energy reflecting your mental creation, which solidifies it and turns it into matter.

They are unaware that action is needed to bring a frequency or consciousness into reality.

By seeking to escape "hard" work, which isn't a necessity unless you deem it so, they escape work all together.

By avoiding the physical, you attempt to go against the structure of reality, which is to go against the structure of yourself, which can only lead to disharmony.

The spiritual planers:

They are unaware that even though they may be connected to God, what they're baking in the oven of God is everything except their desired reality.

Until they become conscious of what they're putting into the oven, they'll keep baking the same reality that they're praying to be rid of.

They are all variations of the same mistake.

PRACTICAL

You must adhere to a specific order to create your desired reality in alignment with the structure of the universe.

The order of alignment goes as follows:

1. Mental plane
2. Spiritual plane
3. Physical plane

The mental and spiritual plane are interchangeable, but the physical is non-negotiable; it must always come last. It is the lowest level of existence. Lowest not meaning lesser value, just that it is not a causal realm.

1. The mental plane

Whatever your desired reality, hold it in mind as if it already exists.

Since the mental plane is the realm of cause, if your desire is to be materialised in reality then you must be operating as if it is already so.

Shift from *desiring* to already *having*. The only way to arrive at the end is to begin at the end.

The mirror will never smile before you do.

2. The spiritual plane

Until you recognise the power within, you will have no power without.

By recognising and internalising that you are a materialisation of God and that God dwells within you, you activate the power of the infinite within you.

There is no greater power in the universe than God, but if you fail to recognise God within you then you will be powerless before any condition, circumstance, event, or person that poses as adversity.

Once you grasp the infinite nature of your true identity, you realise how arrogant it is to think that God could ever fail.

To doubt yourself is to doubt God, which is true blasphemy.

The only way to strengthen yourself on the spiritual plane and to connect to God is to spend more time within than you do without. The vehicle of choice doesn't matter because the destination is the same.

The more time you spend within, the more power you grow within.

The more you cultivate internal power, the less power the external will have over you.

3. The physical plane

Only after arranging yourself correctly on the higher planes of existence can you begin to dominate the lower plane of existence: reality.

Action is unavoidable, but to avoid wasted action the physical plane must come last.

The higher planes of existence metaphysically position you in the correct direction to begin walking towards your desired reality through action.

After vibrationally aligning yourself to your desired reality, you will begin to receive the blueprints on how to physically get there.

REDEFINING MANIFESTATION

PRINCIPLE

 If you desire to change your reality, then you have lost the race before it's even begun.

Manifestation isn't what you think it is.

It's likely that you entered this realm of knowledge seeking to change your reality, but the paradox is that true manifestation has nothing to do with changing reality.

The desire to change reality is actually what keeps so many from ever changing their reality.

True manifestation is solely focused on you, and neglecting reality.

Nothing will ever change until you do you first, and that is a non-negotiable universal truth.

"Indeed, Allāh will not change the condition of a people until they change what is in themselves."

Quran 13:11

The moment you change, the frequency or state of consciousness that the universe picks up from you begins to change, and as a result what is reflected changes.

Think about it in terms of supply and demand.

Every supply is only a product of demand, meaning that the reality you are being supplied with is what you are subconsciously demanding through your frequency or state of consciousness, whether you like it or not.

If you want to be supplied with something different, then you must demand something different, and the unfortunate thing is that we are unaware of what and how we demand.

What you want is not what you demand; what you demand is who you are.

The only thing that the universe will ever recognise as demand is your current frequency or state of consciousness.

You will never change the supply, until you change the demand.

To reiterate initial idea presented at the start of this chapter:

Nothing in your reality will ever change until you change your frequency or state of consciousness.

Your frequency or state of consciousness totals seven keys.

A typical mistake that many make when attempting to alter their reality is to simply alter one or two keys while neglecting the others.

Eventually, the neglected keys unconsciously contradict their change, ultimately contradicting their reality to change.

In the same way that all successful manifestation requires alignment across all three planes of existence, a successful change in frequency requires alignment across all seven keys.

The seven keys to frequency are:

- Beliefs
- Conviction
- Perception
- Emotionally-charged thoughts
- Focus
- Reactions
- Expectations

Your current reality is nothing more than the reflection of what you've been demanding, or in other words, your current beliefs, conviction, attitude, emotionally-charged thoughts, focus, reaction, and expectation.

You have the beliefs equivalent of your current reality, and until you change them you will remain there.

You have the conviction equivalent of your current reality, and until you change it you will remain there.

You have the perception equivalent of your current reality, and until you change it you will remain there.

You have the emotionally-charged thoughts equivalent of your current reality, and until you change them you will remain there.

You have the focus equivalent of your current reality, and until you change it you will remain there.

You have the reactions equivalent of your current reality, and until you change them you will remain there.

You have the expectations equivalent of your current reality, and until you change them you will remain there.

When the seven keys are altered, your frequency is altered. Only then will reality be altered. This can work for you or against you.

When the seven keys are aligned, reality is aligned.

When the seven keys are misaligned, reality is misaligned.

Whether in alignment or not, the universe will always seek to materialise the frequency emitted into reality.

The materialisation of frequency or consciousness into reality is what we call manifestation.

Consciousness and matter are the same energy, only different in rate of vibration; much like steam and ice are the same energy only different in rate of vibration.

Every frequency maintained must and will become a reality, and every reality maintained is nothing more than maintained frequency.

Before we can get to the true essence of manifestation, let's debunk some common myths surrounding it.

1. You don't need to work to manifest.

A lot of "spiritual" people don't realise that they're not seeking anything other than a form of escapism that directly goes against the structure of the universe.

You can't escape physical work any more than you can escape the physical plane.

The notion that you manifest without some sort of physical effort is simply an appeal to an aspect of you that is either exhausted or lazy.

All successful manifestation requires synchronistic alignment across all three planes of existence, not just one or two.

While work is mandatory, hard work is optional but will be made real by your belief in its validity alone.

2. Thoughts create reality

Not all thoughts are equal in their effect over reality.

The only thoughts that have the potential to materialise a reality are those which are emotionally charged.

The true language of the subconscious mind is emotion which also means emotion is the language of God.

Emotion being the language of God means that this is primarily what the universe recognises, and emotion is simply energy in motion which alters the vibration of a thought, making it more powerful and its manifestation more likely.

If there is no emotion behind it, it won't manifest; if there is, it always will.

Emotion is a huge contributor to your frequency, and as a result your reality.

Emotion doesn't necessarily mean a sense of euphoria or excitement, but it is always relative to you as a person. There isn't a one-size-fits-all.

To simplify your understanding, you can think about manifestation like this:

The universe is a sort of warehouse that only delivers the reality that you order. To reiterate, you can only receive what you are asking for (remember, supply and demand).

The issue is, we spend most of our lives consciously asking for one thing, but subconsciously and with our energy asking for another.

Before an order is shipped out, it is identified via a unique product code that the warehouse will match up before distributing.

Think about your frequency like that unique product code that will always match its identical reality before being shipped out.

To reiterate, before anything can exist physically it must first exist vibrationally, which is the combination of mentally and emotionally.

Those who know the true process of manifestation possess the ability to manifest instantly, and that is not an exaggeration.

Before you learn the true process of manifestation, I would like to make something clear:

The knowledge you have is activated by the security you have in the knowledge.

There are individuals with "wrong" knowledge, but through their security and conviction in it, make it right.

There are also individuals with "right" knowledge, but through their insecurity and self-doubt in it, make it wrong.

More important than what you do is the conviction that what you're doing is right.

To act on knowledge while in a state of insecurity and self-doubt will render the potential of the knowledge useless.

Decide that you have everything you need and that you know more than enough to maximise the potential of that knowledge.

The true process of manifestation:

Manifestation is internally shifting to a degree to which you are no longer emotionally dependant on seeing reality change; when you are good with it and good without it.

Diving deeper into this definition can alter everything. There are two layers to this definition:

1. Manifestation is focused on shifting internally, not externally.
2. When you are no longer emotionally dependant on what's going on outside of you, whether positive or negative; when you are good with it and good without it.

PART 1:

The common perception of manifestation is that it's about changing your reality. However, that idea will set you up to continuously fail to manifest or change your reality.

So long as you desire to change your reality, you will be stuck playing the game of reality backwards.

Your purpose for manifesting may be to change your reality, but the process of manifestation requires you to realise the outer world is of no significance and to redirect significance to your inner world only.

To be concerned with the outer world is to be concerned with the effect instead of the cause, a trap that many fall into that puts them in a perpetual cycle of never altering the effect.

You want the effect to be different, but you don't pay any attention to the cause. How can you expect to alter the effect if you fail to alter the cause? This does not make sense.

Manifestation isn't about changing reality, it's only about changing you but so long as you're caught up in changing reality, you're caught up in trying to change an effect by changing an effect, which does not make sense.

With all your focus on the external, you indirectly neglect the internal. As a result, you'll fail to realise that you haven't changed, so how could reality possibly change?

Ironically, the more you seek evidence of reality changing, the more you affirm that you haven't changed, because if you had, there would be no need to look for proof; the change would already be your experience, which is internal.

To be satisfied with yourself but unsatisfied with your reality is paradoxical. It's ignorance of the fact that the two are interconnected which for most is the source of their unwanted reality.

To desire change without change is against the nature of the universe. You can only go somewhere you've never been when you become someone you've never been.

The process of internally shifting is simply the act of exchanging your current state of consciousness for the state of consciousness that matches with your desired reality.

Completely different beliefs, a different level of conviction, a different perception, different emotionally-charged thoughts, different focus, different reactions and different expectations.

PART 2:

If you manifested your desired reality right now, how would you feel?

Happy?

Excited?

Amazing?

Euphoric?

Free?

Relaxed?

Secure?

Accomplished?

If so, that's the exact reason your desired reality will never manifest.

Conversely, if you never manifest your desired reality, how would you feel?

Disappointed?

Crushed?

Sad?

Annoyed?

Frustrated?

Irritated?

Angry?

Empty?

If so, that's the exact reason your desired reality will never manifest.

Whether you realise this is or not, to grant the external the power to alter your internal state is a confession of a dependency on reality.

To be dependent on reality is to require reality to give you what you desire.

Those who are internally dependent on reality will forever be the slave of condition, circumstance, and the events of reality.

To be independent of reality requires you to give yourself what you desire.

Those who are internally independent of reality will never be the slave of condition, circumstance, or events of reality.

The quickest way to determine if you're internally dependent on reality is to ask yourself whether you're postponing the feelings of your desired reality until it manifests.

If that's the case, it means you're waiting for reality to change before allowing yourself to feel those feelings. But in doing so, you reinforce that your reality hasn't changed—so it doesn't.

Ironically, the feelings you envisage as your desired destination are actually the starting point. They generate the frequency that signals to the universe that your desired reality is already yours.

By feeling those emotions now rather than later, you shift your state of consciousness to the present, setting in motion the external changes that reflect your new reality.

The postponement of the emotions you'd feel in your desired reality is the source of your internal dependency on seeing your desired reality, which indirectly shows your ignorance of how reality is materialised. On a deeper level, it is an indication of importance.

Importance to the universe is interpreted as energetic space: the bigger the importance of your desired reality, the bigger the space between you and it; conversely, the smaller the importance of your desired reality, the smaller the space between you and it.

The more you are internally dependent on seeing reality change, the more importance you indicate to the universe, which means the more space there is between you and your desired reality.

If you need your desired reality to materialise before you allow yourself to feel the way you would in that reality, you'll never generate the frequency required to bring it into existence.

The world will never prove anything to you that you have not first proven to yourself.

Internal independence of reality is the essence of what it means to be good with or without it, which is the prerequisite to altering your reality.

Unfortunately, too often you are good with it, but not good without it.

At first, this notion can seem frustrating: how can I be good without it when I need it?

The truth is this notion is liberating. The moment you are no longer dependent on reality, you are freed from it, which also frees up your desired reality to come to you effortlessly.

Your desired reality is merely an aspect of you that already exists within, but it remains imprisoned by your internal dependency on what you believe it will give you.

When reality can offer you nothing, it will offer you everything.

Manifestation has nothing to do with doing, but everything to do with being. It isn't something you need to do; it's something you already do.

Manifestation is like breathing: an effortless, unconscious process. Understanding this is the foundation of all manifestation. Only then will it be experienced as such.

Think about the moments you were searching for a particular car online, and then suddenly you started seeing them everywhere in your reality.

Think about the moments you were searching for some shoes online, and then suddenly you started seeing them everywhere in your reality. Think about the moments you were thinking about someone, and then suddenly they called or texted you.

Manifestation is something you've always done effortlessly; you've never had a problem with it. Truthfully, learning about it is simply discovering what you've been doing forever.

Mistakenly, many desire to "manifest" while negating that they already manifest, then when they fail to "manifest" they conclude they have a problem. Ironically, through their belief in a problem they manifest one.

So rid yourself of your old frequency's trickery, attempting to convince you that you have a problem manifesting. Ironically, there are no truths in reality other than what the subconscious mind accepts as true, so if you believe you will have difficulty manifesting then you shall.

PRACTICAL

Many argue about the best technique for manifesting…

Is it subliminals?

Is it affirmations?

Is it visualization?

Is it vision boards?

Is it writing your goals down as if they are accomplished?

None of these are the best way to materialise your desired reality.

The best manifestation technique is you.

Transcend the infancy of technique or law superiority. The only truth is you; the only law is the law of you.

There is no secret method or technique. One method works for some, others work for others.

Techniques themselves are useless; it is the conviction that you pour into the technique that activates it to work, and nothing else. The technique itself does not create reality. It merely positions you to create your reality by being in the internal state equivalent to your desired reality so it can effortlessly unfold.

The only purpose of these techniques is to internally shift you into the state of consciousness of your desired reality to such a degree you are no longer emotionally dependent on seeing reality change.

Your unwavering conviction that it will work is the only thing that makes it work; that is what activates the technique.

So, to reiterate a point made earlier, more important than what you do is the conviction you have in what you're doing.

Scientists discovered the placebo effect during 18th century, which proves that conviction alone creates change. If you take a sugar pill, truly believing it's medicine, your body responds as if it is because it's not the pill that holds the power, but your conviction in it.

As humans, we are microcosms of the universe. The ancients stated "As above, so below; as below, so above," conveying that we are miniature, walking reflections of the universe. This mean that the universe itself being "so below, as above" has its own placebo effect.

So it's not about affirmations, visualization, vision boards, or writing your goals down as if they're already done. It's about you; that's what it's always been about.

Techniques are like vehicles: it doesn't matter what car you ride in, all that matters is the fuel that's in the vehicle because that will be what drives you to your destination.

In order for a technique to work, using it must generate an intense degree of emotion. To do that, the technique must be vivid. Bear this in mind when choosing your preferred technique.

THE TECHNIQUE I EXCLUSIVELY TEACH CLIENTS

This technique can be used for a number of purposes: to alter an upcoming event such as a job interview, a date, a meeting or simply an uncomfortable conversation. I have seen all the above unfold as desired, including court hearings that were definite jail time.

It can also be used to internally shift you to resonate with the frequency or state of consciousness of your desired reality.

It can also be used to rewrite a traumatic, painful, or upsetting past event that still may have a grasp on you to this day.

This method capitalises on the fact that the mind cannot distinguish between fact and imagination or consciousness. When imagination becomes real to the mind, it alters your frequency or state of consciousness to reflect that, causing reality to reorganise itself in alignment with your internal shift.

This technique has the sole purpose of convincing your mind that what you are experiencing within is real, and it will only accept it as real if what you are experiencing within generates an intense degree of emotion and is vivid.

An intense degree of emotion may mean euphoria, it may mean tears of joy, it may mean extreme gratitude, it may mean uncontainable excitement, it may mean deep peace, it may mean complete serenity. It is entirely dependent on how you would be upon attaining your desired reality; it is not one size fits all.

I am rarely excited but often extremely calm, so that is the emotion that resonates my truth.

Vivid implies clarity, which means knowing exactly what you want with pinpoint precision so there is no room for confusion.

These two components combined will be sufficient to convince the mind that the internal experience is something that has actually been experienced. It will then begin resonating with the frequency aligned to what you desire, setting in motion the materialisation of that frequency into reality.

As mentioned earlier, importance is the enemy of the materialisation of your desired reality. The beauty of internally, intensely, and vividly experiencing your desired reality within through this technique is that the more you do it, the more your mind accepts that this has already happened, which decreases the external desire and importance placed upon on it.

The only way to reduce the importance placed upon your desired reality is experiencing it internally because then, and only then, shall it no longer be desired externally, which aligns you with it.

Your desired reality is only important because you don't have it, and if you did, it wouldn't be important.

Too many see their desired reality as a pair of shoes in the shop window, instead of the pair they already own and have been wearing for months.

The importance you give to a desired reality is an indication of internally lacking the frequency equivalent of that desired reality; you only want it because you don't have it.

Using this technique correctly positions you to take your desired reality for granted.

At first, this notion may seem confusing, but that is only until we look to human nature for understanding. As humans, unfortunately, it is within our nature to take for granted that which we have. By taking your desired reality for granted, you indirectly indicate to the universe that you already have it.

Think about how everything you currently take for granted comes to you effortlessly.

This does not contradict the notion that any technique you use must generate an intense degree of emotion. The purpose of this is to generate a frequency aligned to your desired reality.

Fortunately, the natural side effect of intensely and internally feeling the emotions you'd feel in your desired reality is a reduced desire for it externally; in effect, killing two birds with one stone.

The technique I exclusively teach to clients is simple and made up of two parts: the isolated practice of visualization, and carrying that internal shift into your daily life.

PART ONE

1. Clearly define the circumstance, event or reality that you desire. There must be no confusion about what you want to manifest.

2. Sit or lie down until you reach a state of deep relaxation and stillness. Whether this takes five, 10, 20, or even 40 minutes doesn't matter; being relaxed is mandatory.

    -   Clarification: You'll know you're relaxed enough when your body feels loose, heavy, or weightless, and your mind becomes quieter. If you still feel restless, take more time.

3. Imagine a scene that includes someone who cares for you: a friend, partner, or family member who recognises your desire by commenting on it in a natural and personal way.

    -   Clarification: If you don't have someone who would naturally comment on your success, use a person you admire, a role model, or even a past version of yourself reflecting on the achievement.

- If your desired reality isn't something others would comment on (e.g. internal growth), imagine a scene where they acknowledge your transformation through a change in your energy, demeanour, or actions.

4. Include physical touch in the scene: a high five, fist bump, hug, or anything that feels natural with them and intimate.

5. Keep the scene short, focusing only on their comments on your desired reality materialising, and replay it again and again on a continuous loop.

- Clarification: The scene is kept short to prevent overcomplication. If it's too long, your focus will scatter. Keep it concise and impactful.

- To make the loop feel natural, imagine it like a movie clip replaying; fading out then seamlessly restarting.

6. If imagined vividly, you will naturally begin to feel the emotions you'd experience upon your desired reality materializing. Feel these deeply.

- Clarification: If emotions don't come easily, focus on amplifying the details: tone of voice, expressions, warmth of touch. Emotion is triggered by immersion into vividness, so sink deeper into the scene.

7. There is no set time for this practice. The moment you begin to feel strain, effort, or fatigue, stop immediately.

   - Clarification: If you notice yourself forcing it, don't push through. Ease out of it naturally and return to it another time.

PART TWO

1. Pick a single, simple sentence that you would naturally say to yourself upon your desire manifesting. It must be authentic: what you'd truly think or say.

   - Clarification: If you struggle to come up with a natural sentence, imagine seeing your desired reality unfold right now in front of you: what's the first thought that runs through your mind? That's your sentence.

2. What is the feeling you'd experience naturally and exclusively upon your desired reality materializing? Clearly define it.

3. Repeat the sentence in your head continuously throughout the day, feeling what you would feel if it were already your reality.

   - Clarification: You don't need to say it out loud, just think it – like an internal affirmation.

If you struggle to feel the right emotion, slow down and focus. Instead of repeating the sentence mechanically, imagine the depth behind it.

There's no need to force constant repetition. If you forget to do it at times, that doesn't ruin the process. Just return to it whenever you remember.

This isn't about repeating the sentence mindlessly all day but about anchoring yourself in the feeling whenever possible.

If your mood fluctuates throughout the day, don't panic; shifting states is natural. Simply return to the sentence and feeling without resistance.

In both aspects of the technique, simplicity is mandatory.

Techniques can be used every day, but not for the sake of creation as they do not create. They must only be used to internally experience the state of consciousness you desire.

Do not make a chore out of it, as this perception will eventually lead to feeling obliged, bordering on resentment, which will emit a frequency that will negatively alter the frequency of your desired reality.

If it's beginning to feel like a chore, take a break and enjoy your reality.

Here are some examples of how the technique can be applied to different desired realities.

The Desire for Love

Part one: visualised scene – A close friend or family member hugging you while saying, "This is the love you've always deserved; you're so happy." Or however your friend or family member would say it.

Part two: mental affirmation – "I'm finally in the relationship I've always wanted to be in."

The Desire for a Specific Job

Part one: visualised scene – A close friend or family member hugging you while saying, "Congratulations, I knew you were gonna get the job!" Or however your friend or family member would say it.

Part two: mental affirmation – "I'm so grateful I got this job."

The Desire for a Specific Income

Part one: visualised scene – A close friend or family member hugging you while saying, "I can't believe you're making that much; that's insane!" Or however your friend or family member would say it.

Part two: mental affirmation – "Now I have more money than I can spend."

The Desire for a Specific Physique

Part one: visualised scene – A close friend or family member hugging you while saying, "You look like you live in the gym these days; you gotta train me!" Or however your friend or family member would say it.

Part two: mental affirmation – "I'm in the best shape of my life."

The Desire for Business Success

Part one: visualised scene – A close friend or family member hugging you while saying, "Congratulations, how does it feel to be making X amount of money!" Or however your friend or family member would say it.

Part two mental affirmation – "Sales are coming in like crazy these days."

These are just some examples – adapt them to your specific desire.

All Manifestation Is Instant

When aiming to materialise your desired reality, it's natural to ask: "How long will it take to manifest what I want?"

This question is a confession of ignorance to the true essence of manifestation. Remember, manifestation isn't a matter of altering reality; it's about altering oneself.

Altering oneself can happen in an instant, which would mean that all manifestations are instant.

The act of altering reality requires a transcendence of third-dimensional constraint, one of those constraints being time. You need to transcend time by immersing yourself within the state of consciousness of your desired reality. By doing so, you experience the truest essence of your desired reality.

Those who think manifestation is about altering reality will always wait for reality to be altered, which indirectly indicates to the universe they are lacking what they desire.

Imagine your desired reality as a jacket: from the moment you step into its frequency or state of consciousness, you "put on" the jacket, and you remain in that state until you unconsciously choose to "take it off," which is when you shift out of that frequency or state of consciousness.

Once you have truly entered the state of consciousness or frequency of your desired reality, you will not need to see reality change. So "how long" or "when" will not even be relevant; if it is, that is an indication that you must internally, intensely, and vividly experience your desired reality more.

There Are No Big or Small Manifestations

Nothing in the universe is bigger than God, but paradoxically whatever God deems bigger will be.

Big or small are concepts that do not exist to the infinite.

It is us defining that leads to confining. Your perception of a reality will always lead to the projection of a reality.

If you view your desired reality as big, then it will be too big for you to materialise; not because it is big, but because you have made it so.

Often, the difficulty of materialising our desired reality does not lay in the reality, but in our unawareness of how we make it difficult.

To the infinite, the reality that you so greatly desire is no greater than the one you currently experience, and vice versa. It is all the same since it is above duality.

It seems as though whatever we deem to be big becomes too big for our minds to conceive us materialising, so the wise thing to do would be to deem your desired reality as small.

By deeming it small, it isn't too big for your mind to conceive materialising, which allows for a smooth materialisation of your desired reality.

You Need to Build Manifestation Muscle

Manifestation, despite being something you already do, operates in a similar way to a skill.

There are individuals who seem to have the ability to materialise whatever it is they want, and the source of their power lies in their manifestation muscle.

Some people have weak manifestation muscle and others have strong manifestation muscle, which makes all the difference.

Manifestation works like building muscle in the gym.

The more you materialise, the stronger your "manifestation muscle" becomes.

If you're trying to manifest something too big, too soon, without proper "training" or building up smaller wins, you risk feeling stuck in a cycle of failure.

Just like you wouldn't try to lift extremely heavy weights without training, you shouldn't expect to manifest huge desires without gradually working your way up.

Manifestation muscle is nothing more than a measurement of conviction you have in your ability to materialise your desires. The more you see evidence of your ability to manifest, the more that strengthens your conviction; and the more conviction you have, the more and the easier you're able to manifest.

It's likely that you don't have sufficient conviction in your ability to alter reality. That's not because you can't manifest; it is because you neglect the instances you do manifest.

Remember, you have been manifesting on autopilot your whole life; by becoming aware that you are already manifesting, you recognise the invisible string that connects reality and your mind. The more evidence you see, the more conviction you have and the more muscle you gain.

Often, we do not realise that we have the conviction necessary to materialise our desired reality. A recommended way to build conviction is by materialising what you deem to be "small" things. The mind will naturally note these instances as evidence, which quickly stacks up.

Manifest seeing a specific pair of shoes.

Manifest seeing a specific car in a specific colour.

Manifest seeing a specific-coloured backpack.

Manifest an available parking space.

Each small success builds confidence, strengthens your conviction, and makes it easier to manifest bigger goals over time.

Building manifestation muscle requires patience, consistency, and incremental progress. After a while, your mind will naturally have a shortcut and the idea of your desired reality will seem easy.

That is everything you need to know when it comes to manifestation. There is no other secret key or hidden ancient wisdom you are missing; you have it all, as you always have.

I'd like to end this chapter by saying that manifestation is not you creating reality. There is nothing for you to create since all realities and frequencies already exist within the infinite within. Manifestation isn't creation; it is revelation.

You are revealing what already exists within.

THE DESIRE OF YOUR DESIRES

PRINCIPLE

Just let go.

Just detach.

These are not new concepts, yet they seem so difficult to do.

How can I detach from wanting more money when I need to pay my bills?

How can I detach from wanting a romantic partner when I need love?

How can I detach from my career when I need to progress?

Detachment and letting go are necessary if you are to alter your reality. But they cannot be unlocked unless you understand exactly what this means.

You will never be able to let go or detach unless you know what you truly want.

You don't want what you think you want. Until you realise what you truly want, you will not be in a reality where you experience what you want.

It's likely that you are reading this book because you want to materialise a reality of success, prosperity, health, love, abundance, and good fortune. This is your first mistake…

So long as your motive is to change your reality, you're playing the game backwards. It's not about reality, and it never has been.

Paradoxically, again, none of this is truly about changing reality; it's about changing you.

When your focus is locked on fixing or controlling reality, you end up neglecting yourself.

And in neglecting yourself, you unknowingly continue to create the very reality you're trying to escape.

Everybody wants to change their reality one way or another, whether they want:

- a romantic partner
- better looks
- material abundance
- a specific career
- more money
- a specific house
- a specific car

- a specific holiday
- better health
- a life of freedom

We want things, and that's the issue.

Most people spend their lives wanting things, without things wanting them.

The people who have the things you desire, whether consciously or unconsciously, know how to make those things want them. Until you know how, you'll want forever but never be wanted.

If you hear the whispers of reality, you don't need to hear the screams; the workings of the universe have never been hidden from you.

It's easier to make a cheetah come to you than it is to chase a cheetah.

It's easier to make a butterfly come to you than it is to chase a butterfly.

It's easier to make a fish come to you than it is to chase a fish.

You're focusing on the wrong thing; you don't want what you think you want.

You don't want that person; you don't want that amount of money; you don't want that house; you don't want that trip; you don't want that career.

Big or small, you don't want anything that you think you want, but because you think you do, that's where all your energy is focused and as a result, wasted.

For anything you ever want in life, remember this:

You don't want what you "desire" but the internal state you believe it would put you in.

Here are some examples to illustrate the point:

You don't want a toothpick for the sake of wanting a toothpick, you want to be in comfort.

You don't want a drink for the sake of wanting a drink, you want to quench your thirst and feel satisfied.

You don't want a person for the sake of wanting a person, you want to be appreciated, seen, loved, and cherished, or sexually satisfied.

You don't want a house for the sake of wanting a house, you want to feel accomplished, proud, and secure.

You don't want more money for the sake of wanting more money, you want to feel secure, free, and relieved.

You don't want the things themselves; you want how the things would make you feel.

If they didn't change how you felt, you wouldn't want them.

Whether the feeling is mild or strong, we still want it. If you dig deep enough, at the root of everything you'll ever want you will find a frequency that you believe is missing.

All we want in life is frequency.

We were once interconnected and part of the infinite, but through materialising ourselves on this physical plane we separated to a degree, and so every desire we have is nothing more than a feeble attempt to become whole again.

You don't want anything in this world even though you've become convinced that you do. What you want is a different state of consciousness than the one you have now.

How can you expect to detach from the world when what you think you want is the world? It's a trap.

This is why the notion of letting go or detaching makes sense intellectually but not practically. Until your concept of what you desire changes, nothing will change.

You will never want something in reality without reason. Reason is meaning, and meaning is always emotional, which poses a question:

How do you think you'd feel upon materialising what you want?

If you can answer that question, you can have what you want.

And this leads us to the paradox of reality: the universe interprets you wanting something as an indication that you don't have it.

How can you want something that you already have?

You only want that house because you don't have it.

You only want that career because you don't have it.

You only want that person because you don't have them.

You only want more money because you don't have enough.

This is how the universe thinks.

In this universe, there are two chairs: wanting and having.

You can't sit in two chairs at once; you're either in one or the other.

Anytime that you want something, the universe registers that you don't have it, and that is what's reflected, leading to a continual cycle of you wanting but never receiving.

To want is to decline what you could have.

Wanting something will repel you from ever having it.

Having must be understood through the lens of the universe rather than the human definition.

Having to humans and to the universe are two completely different things.

For humans, having refers to physically possessing.

On a universal level, having refers to vibrationally possessing.

We humans want our desires because we physically don't have them, and if we did then we wouldn't want them anymore because we'd already have them.

To the universe, the physical plane is an illusion; it's insignificant as it isn't grounded in universal truth.

The universe, knowing that reality is merely an illusion, doesn't revere it as we do. What it truly honours and responds to is vibration, because vibration is the cause, the source and the truth behind the illusion.

Only what is vibrationally possessed is real to the universe because that vibration will eventually compound into frequency, which must become reality.

Vibrational possession refers to your current mental and emotional state, which aligns with a frequency that aligns with a reality.

If you want all your desires to be met on a human level, you must have them on a universal level.

To revisit the point made at the beginning of this chapter, it's about shifting away from reality and towards your internal state; it's never been about reality.

To vibrationally possess what you want, you must have it, and you have it the moment you occupy the mental attitude/frequency/state of consciousness/internal state of it.

It's not about changing reality; it's about you giving you what you think you've been missing that you've had within you and will always have to the end of time.

You think getting what you want will make you feel a certain way, without realising that feeling that certain way will get you what you want because you have it.

Use the technique already given.

Ironically, the more you immerse yourself in feeling how you'd feel upon attaining your desired reality, the less you need it externally, and that's how you detach or let go.

That's the lightbulb moment that some will never experience.

They will chase the career, the looks, the partners, and the money without realising they're running in the wrong direction; the more they run, the further and further they stray from what's truly real, which is within.

Detachment can only take place when you detach from what doesn't truly exist.

Letting go can only take place when you let go from what doesn't truly exist.

HOW TO KNOW EXACTLY WHAT ACTION TO TAKE

PRINCIPLE

You may still be asking: what action do I need to take to manifest my desired reality?

How do I act?

When do I act?

The blueprint of your desired reality exists within you.

Imagine if you had instructions from the version of you in your desired reality on exactly what to do to get there in the most efficient and effortless way.

From the perspective of infinite parallel universes, the version of you living in your desired reality isn't just a wish or goal; it's a reality that already exists.

Another way of conceptualizing it is to understand that the essence of everything is within you, which means *all* frequencies and *all* realities are also within you.

Whether through the lens of quantum physics or spirituality, everything that you'll ever need and ever want is already within you, simply waiting to be accessed.

The guidance and instructions are ready and waiting, but first you need to know the multi-dimensional sequence.

That's when you'll know exactly what to do.

The mistake that most make is acting on a frequency contradictory to their desired reality.

The wrong frequency even with the right action will always lead to the wrong reality.

The wrong state of consciousness even with the right action will always lead to the wrong reality.

In a battle between actions and frequency, frequency wins every time.

You cannot and will not outhustle your frequency.

The masses live in frequencies that are contradictory to their desired reality. They spend their life senselessly taking action to get to their desired realities, without ever realising that action doesn't create reality, only frequency does.

They are like flies trying to get outside through a closed window; they desperately want to escape so they continuously bash into the window with all their might, burning themselves out and eventually dying on the window sill.

Taking action to become wealthy while being in the frequency of poverty will only lead to a reality of poverty.

No action from poverty will ever bring wealth.

Taking action to become fit while in the frequency of being unfit will only lead to a reality of unfitness.

No action from unfitness will ever bring fitness.

Taking action to become free while being in the frequency of survival will only lead to a reality of survival.

No action from survival mode will ever bring freedom.

Action alone isn't enough, but it is a necessity.

Since you exist in a physical world it cannot be avoided, but that doesn't mean the action you take must be hard. You act through your ego, also known as your physical vessel, that relies on its five senses to navigate and make sense of the world.

The ego isolates itself from the infinite intelligence and as a result suffers from a limited awareness of the entirety of reality, seeing everything from the lowest level of consciousness.

Seeing everything from the lowest level limits results to be of the lowest level, and this is where most of humanity will reside for the rest of their lives.

To the ego, action leads to results.

Think about it:

Whenever you want something, you take action to get it.

Whenever you want to go somewhere, you take action to get there.

Whenever you want to eat something, you take action to eat it.

Whenever you want to drink something, you take action to drink it.

But remember, the ego operates from a limited awareness of reality, so it doesn't know what is really going on.

When the ego experiences something it doesn't like, it fixates on the process of taking action to change the result.

The illusion presented here by the ego is a trap, that you can change an effect by changing the effect itself.

Actions and the subsequent results or changes exist within the physical plane, which is the realm of effect.

All actions, results or changes are nothing more than effects themselves and not causes, which means they had already been long set in motion before they are experienced.

This is why action alone will never alter reality; maybe momentarily but never completely.

The only way to change an effect is to change the cause.

The multi-dimensional sequence from which action originates is as follows:

Consciousness/Frequency -> Intuition -> Mental Nudges -> Action -> Reality

Until you understand this, like the masses you will continue to act senselessly and it will never be enough.

Let's begin with the end product, which is reality.

To get there, we take action. Think of action as the midwife of energy, solidifying the immaterial to the material.

We take action based upon small mental nudges that compel us to do something.

Whether taking a different route, reaching out to someone, sorting out documents, changing this or buying that, we all experience these mental nudges. They are subtle, but they direct us on what to do.

The mental nudges that we experience are a direct result of our intuition.

Intuition is an amalgamation of two words, inner and tuition, meaning guidance or teaching that comes from within.

The mental nudges that you receive that compel you to take specific action is directly reflective of your intuition. If intuition is what we download, then every download has a source, and that source is frequency. Your frequency will determine the download you extract.

Frequency has a domino effect across the multi-dimensional sequence of events that lead to action. Since it is the highest level, it has the most power.

Let's now revisit one of the examples listed earlier with an understanding of the sequence:

Taking action to become wealthy while being in the frequency of poverty will only lead to a reality of poverty.

No action from poverty will ever bring wealth.

Frequency (Poverty) -> Intuition (Poverty) -> Mental Nudges (Poverty) -> Action (Poverty) -> Reality (Poverty)

If someone is tuned into a frequency of poverty, that will determine their intuition, meaning they can only download information from a source of poverty. This leads to mental nudges that reflect poverty, causing action towards poverty, ultimately creating a reality reflective of poverty.

Taking the action to reach a reality of being fit while being in the frequency of being unfit will only lead to a reality of unfit.

No action from unfitness will ever bring fitness.

Frequency (Unfitness) -> Intuition (Unfitness) -> Mental Nudges (Unfitness) -> Action (Unfitness) -> Reality (Unfitness)

Somebody tuned in a frequency of unfitness can only experience an intuition that downloads information from a source of unfitness, leading to mental nudges that will eventually reflect unfitness, leading to action built off these mental nudges of unfitness ultimately reflecting a reality of unfitness.

Taking the action to reach a reality of freedom while being in the frequency of survival will only lead to a reality of survival.

No action from survival mode will ever bring freedom.

Frequency (Survival) -> Intuition (Survival) -> Mental Nudges (Survival) -> Action (Survival) -> Reality (Survival)

Somebody tuned in a frequency of survival can only experience an intuition that downloads information from a source of survival, leading to mental nudges that will eventually reflect survival, leading to action built off these mental nudges of survival ultimately reflecting a reality of survival. Most spend their lives attempting to fight against the tide of the universe, which is their own state of consciousness or frequency.

The multi-dimensional sequence from which action originates cannot be violated. Every and any attempt to do so will only result in frustration and failure.

You must comply with how the universe works in order for things to work for you.

When you work so hard and it is still not enough, it's easy to experience frustration, irritation, and apathy. The unfortunate irony is that these are all emotions that lead to the output of a frequency that the universe will then magnify, making you feel more frustrated, irritated, and apathetic while you're working so hard.

But to the same degree that the multi-dimensional sequence from which action originates can work against you, it can work for you.

Now that you understand the sequence from the top down, instead of spending your time at the bottom like so many, you can alter it from the top. The knock-on effect is that you know exactly how to change your reality.

As mentioned, frequency ultimately determines the intuition you download, the mental nudges that you receive and the mental nudges that are physically executed, so we must shift from operating on the lowest level of consciousness to the highest level of consciousness.

The moment you alter your frequency, it has a ripple effect through the sequence that alters the action you take.

So long as your frequency is calibrated to your desired reality, this will lead to you being internally guided by the version of you in your desired reality via the intuition into which you can tune, leading to mental nudges that come from the version of you in your desired reality, leading to action that comes from the version of you in your desired reality that finally leads to your desired reality manifesting.

This is the same in theory and actuality.

By shifting into the frequency or state of consciousness of your desired reality and operating from it, you can be guided on exactly how to get there.

What you consider your destination is actually your starting location; you can only be wherever you already are.

Consciousness/Frequency (Desired Reality) -> Intuition (Desired Reality) -> Mental Nudges (Desired Reality) -> Action (Desired Reality) -> Reality (Desired Reality)

Something important to note: being in the frequency of your desired reality is only as valuable as your ability to tune into your intuition and then execute upon your mental nudges.

The world programmes us to second guess ourselves. In school, teachers checking our work can lead to the idea that what we do is inadequate and requires external validation, leading to an unconscious degree of self-distrust.

A pattern of external verification and validation is set in motion, so we hesitate to trust ourselves, spending our whole lives wanting to be guided or validated.

If you don't trust yourself then how can you guide yourself?

Do you trust yourself?

Only you can answer this. Remember, you can lie to everybody except the universe.

The degree to which you trust yourself determines your ability to capitalise on the frequency you're seeking to bring from the immaterial to the material.

If you don't trust yourself, you won't trust your intuition, which means you won't trust the mental nudges that you download, making everything pointless.

Many claim to trust God but do not even trust themselves.

How well can anyone trust God if they do not trust themselves?

You can be in the right frequency, that which reflects your desired reality, but without self-trust you won't be able to materialise it.

If you don't trust yourself then how can the universe trust you?

Self-trust is crucial.

The more self-trust you have, the more and the quicker you'll be able to transform frequency into reality.

PRACTICAL

These downloads are like schools of fish; abundant, yes, but they can easily slip away and you don't know when the next one will come along.

If you allow a mental nudge from your desired reality to slip away, you risk falling out of the frequency of your desired reality through life's ups and downs.

If that happens, the wrong fish will start swimming by. You risk potentially executing upon mental nudges not aligned to the frequency of your desired reality.

The speed that you execute these mental nudges with will reflect the amount of self-trust and conviction that you have, ultimately setting in motion for it to be compounded. After tuning into the frequency of your desired reality, it's likely that you will be guided to do things you haven't done before or that you've been meaning to do but about which you have been procrastinating.

Procrastination is simply the stagnation of energy caused by trying to take action contradictory to your frequency.

Once your frequency is aligned with the action you're trying to take, you'll naturally be compelled to act.

The frequency of your desired reality will bring you to your desired reality so long as you can bring yourself to do what you are being nudged to do.

It will be subtle at first as it's likely you haven't been listening, but the more you listen and the more you do as it directs you the louder and clearer it will become.

At first, the mental nudges of your desired reality will feel uncomfortable and somewhat foreign, but that's simply because you're leaving your old frequency, otherwise known as your comfort zone. It will feel different, but that indicates an energetic shift.

Here are a couple of examples of differences that may arise once you shift into the frequency of your desired reality:

- Apply for that job.
- Change your website or social media profile.
- Reach out to someone you've been meaning to contact.
- Start that diet.
- Buy that book.
- Go a different route than normal.
- Tell someone how you truly feel.

- Work on something you've been meaning to do.

- Pivot strategy.

- Quit your job or business.

- Break-up with someone.

- Sort out your email inbox.

The moment you're tuned into the frequency of your desired reality, rest assured that you will know what to do. You can even convince yourself now that you know what to do and follow the guidance from within.

Prepare to be guided to act differently and quickly.

To metaphysically position yourself to walk effortlessly into your desired reality, remember this phrase:

Frequency first, action after.

THE PERCEPTION PROJECTION LOOP

PRINCIPLE

What you stare into is staring back at you and eventually will become you.

The way you look at reality is the way reality will look back at you, and that's simply because you and reality are one.

The masses will look out into their world without realising they are simply looking in their world.

Many see a reality they don't like without ever realising they are not seeing reality, but their distorted version of reality.

As human beings, we are comforted by the notion that when we look out into the world, we are seeing it as it is, without ever realising a deep metaphysical truth…

You don't see the world as it is, but as you are.

You don't realise that you are seeing reality through lenses tinted by your state of consciousness or frequency. This applies to everyone.

Perception is defined in the *Cambridge Dictionary* as a belief or opinion, often held by many people and based on how things seem.

There's two important parts to that definition. Until you unpack them, you will continue in a cycle of unwanted reality:

1. "A belief or opinion."
2. "Based on how things seem."

A belief or opinion aren't truths; they're ideas that mask themselves as truths.

However, once accepted by the subconscious mind they begin to become truths by materialising all around us in our realities.

There are no truths in your reality other than what your subconscious accepts as true. Once accepted, this truth will solidify.

How things seem will always depend on where you are standing – I'm not talking about your physical position but your mental one: your state of consciousness or your frequency.

By dissecting the definition of perception, a truth is revealed: your perception ultimately leads to your projection, which is what we call reality.

Most people will never realise that the way they are choosing to perceive something is intricately connected to the reality that their mind projects.

The dangerous thing about perception being connected to projection is that it is the beginning of a cycle from which many will never escape: the "perception-projection loop."

Unaware that the way they see reality is the way it sees them, most people take a dim view of reality, which can only lead to them projecting the worst.

The most unfortunate part about this is that once they experience the worst, unaware that it's closely related to how they are seeing reality, they champion that experience as truth, further reinforcing and solidifying that reality (perception).

Perception drugs you with an artificial ego boost. All humans love being right, sometimes even if it leads to our own destruction.

Yet, in these circumstances, the irony is that they are wrong, as it is only a truth in the subconscious mind. It is common in dating circles for people to bemoan a lack of suitable potential partners.

That perception ultimately leads to a projection of reality. They go on a succession of bad dates with people they don't get on with, leading them to them to believe they were right.

They don't realise that their desire to be proven right is sabotaging their dates, destroying any chance of them finding love.

Your perception quite literally causes you to emit a different frequency, ultimately putting you in a completely different world, one of many.

Perception will act blindly. It can either help or harm you. It is a tool of construction or destruction.

If your perception doesn't serve you, then it will control you. There are two things that'll cause this:

1. The old frequency

The main aim of your old frequency is to exist, and perception is one way it continues projecting its frequency into your current reality.

When you experience certain conditions, events, circumstances, or people, it'll immediately encourage you to look at situation through the worst lens possible. As a result, you create the worst outcome possible.

After creating the worst outcome, it's natural to feel and think the worst thing possible.

That mental and emotional energy is getting its fix.

2. The world

The universe seeks balance. It prefers everything to operate on a similar level for its own equilibrium. But that balance only exists if everyone remains at the same level of consciousness.

To maintain this, society feeds us the same set of beliefs: the widely accepted "truths" about how life works, what's possible, and what isn't.

And the irony? The world sells you these beliefs once, and then you spend the rest of your life reselling them to yourself.

Unfortunately, it sells us the version it wants us to live in, which revolves around failure, limitation, misery, suffering, scarcity, and struggle.

Once a belief is accepted, it becomes the lens through which you see the world. That ultimately shapes your reality, so it is your reality.

It is often said that "perception is reality," and metaphysically it is.

If you see the world through your own lens which shapes the projection of your reality, it would be wise to perceive your life through the lens of your desired reality, so you can experience the projection of that reality.

Every circumstance, condition, event, or experience with people in your reality must be seen through this lens.

PRACTICAL

If the version of me in my desired reality jumped into my body, how would it look at things?

There is no right or wrong answer. The purpose of the framing is simply to flex the perception muscle of your desired reality. The more you see reality through this lens, the more reality will see you that way.

Changing reality is simply a matter of changing how the world sees you. In order to change the way the world sees you, you must change the way you see yourself. You must change the way you see through yourself.

At the beginning, this process will require some conscious practice, but eventually it will become unconscious. At that point, the manifestation will feel effortless.

Control your perception or the world will control it for you.

YOU DON'T HAVE BELIEFS, THEY HAVE YOU

PRACTICAL

It is arrogant of humanity to think that we possess beliefs. The humble truth is that beliefs possess us.

If you want to understand your beliefs, look what you believe or know to be true of the world.

If you ask the average person on the street to tell you what they believe about the world, they'll either not be able to tell you or proclaim that it's the truth. This is the point of my statement; for the most part, our beliefs are invisible.

All beliefs seek to convince us that they are truths rather than simply beliefs.

In reality, there are no truths other than what the subconscious mind accepts as true, because what it does believe to be true will be projected and experienced in reality.

As humans, what we regard as truth is simply what we've experienced, and what we've experienced is nothing more than the materialisation of our frequency.

Foundationally, a belief is simply an idea based upon the potential of an infinite number of realities, not an actuality.

All beliefs are living entities. As living entities, all beliefs want energy.

Once you see that beliefs operate like entities, it all makes sense.

Since there are an infinite number of potential realities, there are an infinite number of beliefs, and all those beliefs are fighting for our attention because that is what brings them into existence.

Beliefs want the energy to materialise further through seeking emotion combined with conviction.

Beliefs don't serve you; they serve themselves. They will attempt to convince you that they are truths, but they are simply ideas pretending to be truths.

The unfortunate thing is that when a belief has reached "truth" status, it has accumulated so much energy that attempting to remove it will almost feel like insanity and stupidity, because "it's the truth." This is its in-built defence mechanism.

Typically, beliefs are defined as thoughts that you keep thinking, but that's insufficient because you can keep thinking something all day and it won't materialise.

Anything that materialises in reality first existed in the subconscious mind, and the entry requirement to the subconscious mind is emotion.

Hence why, for simplicity, I define a belief as a singular thought or a multitude of thoughts that have emotion and conviction behind them.

You will always find emotion lurking around a belief. If emotion begins to surface when you attack a belief, you've hit the jackpot.

Since emotion solidifies belief, it is also what holds the belief in the subconscious mind. As a protective mechanism, the belief will release emotion when it feels threatened so we feel discomfort then decide to leave it alone.

Observe when someone's view on the world is questioned and they begin to feel upset, angry, or disrespected; that's the belief, not them.

In the realm of psychology this phenomenon is called cognitive dissonance, and that is when one's belief has merged into one's identity to such a degree that when the belief is attacked, the same areas of the brain responsible for identity light up as if being attacked.

Understanding that we are all microcosms of the universe, on a metaphysical level beliefs attach themselves to us to such a degree that we can't differentiate between them. They want to present the illusion that they've merged with us, so we unconsciously accept this and experience it in our reality.

Beliefs are masters of illusion and continuously will attempt to trick you into feeling as if you have no control over them, and that they're something above you.

Most people feel imprisoned by self-limiting beliefs, when the truth is that all beliefs are self-limiting. A belief is simply an emotionally-fixed perspective, a mental construct that defines reality in a particular way.

All beliefs create boundaries around what you can experience in reality.

The individual who thinks they must work hard for money has now created a boundary outside of which they are unable to experience.

But how often does it feel like we simply can't change our beliefs?

They feel like mental boulders, something we have no power over. This is part of the trick.

Remember that beliefs want to stay. That's all they want to do; stay in your mind to get as much energy as possible, so they have the chance of materialising.

So beliefs will present the illusion that they are unchangeable.

Ironically, because there are no truths other than what the subconscious mind accepts as true, when you believe a certain belief is unchangeable, it becomes unchangeable.

Ironically, because there are no truths other than what the subconscious mind accepts as true, when you believe it's hard to change a certain belief, it becomes hard.

Ironically, because there are no truths other than what the subconscious mind accepts as true, when you believe a certain belief is the absolute truth, it becomes the absolute truth.

Beliefs sell you this illusion that they are unmovable, and the moment you buy into that belief, sold to you by the con artist itself, then reality will be unmovable; not because it is, but because you have decided it is so.

More important than what you believe you need to change in reality is your beliefs about beliefs.

How can you change your beliefs on money if you don't think you can change your beliefs on beliefs?

How can you change your beliefs on relationships if you don't think you can change your beliefs on beliefs?

How can you change your beliefs on people if you don't think you can change your beliefs on beliefs?

How can you change your beliefs on success if you don't think you can change your beliefs on beliefs?

I can assure you, it'll be hard to change to your beliefs so long as you think it's hard. Nobody ever seems to decide straight away that it's easy to change their beliefs.

Decide that the truth is that no belief is unchangeable.

Decide that the truth is that no belief is the absolute truth.

Decide that the truth is that no belief is unmovable.

By making this obvious yet abstract change, the clay of your mind de-solidifies ready for your moulding.

Which brings us to a hidden truth about all beliefs: they are simply choices that at some point, whether conscious or unconscious, right or wrong, forced or accepted, we make.

Changing a belief is simply making the conscious decision to believe something else. There's nothing more to it than that. It is just a decision.

But it doesn't feel so simple, does it? It feels as though that's not enough. It feels as though it's more complicated. It feels as though it should be more profound.

Notice the key word there? *Feels.*

Remember that beliefs protect themselves with emotion.

Why should changing your beliefs be complex?

Why isn't that simple decision to believe something else enough?

Why does it have to be more complicated?

Why should it feel groundbreaking?

Where did you get the idea that is has to be complex, complicated, and groundbreaking?

Your acceptance of those ideas is the only thing maintaining those ideas.

The ego thrives on intellectual superiority, finding validation in complexity. Solving something intricate feels satisfying; cracking a difficult problem feels like genius; and uncovering a groundbreaking revelation brings euphoria.

This is why the mind is drawn to complexity; it feeds the ego's desire to feel special and accomplished.

What do you want? Do you want intellectual superiority or your desired reality?

Assuming you picked the latter, then accept that all it takes to change a belief is simply making the conscious decision to believe something else.

The something else you believe in has to reflect your desired reality.

The beliefs that you currently have are producing your current reality, so to experience to a new reality, you must begin to adopt beliefs you've never had.

All beliefs have two origin points: experience and adoption.

1. Experience

The moment we experience something in reality, our mind internalises that experience as truth, and it is, but we fail to realise that it is only because it was first a truth in the mind.

The physical plane, or what we call reality, is nothing more than a delayed creation of our consciousness, or a reflection of the mental plane which is our mind.

We think we gain our beliefs from reality, but reality is gained from our beliefs.

We experience the effect, never taking into consideration the cause of the effect, and the cause is always intertwined with deciding to accept our beliefs.

I'll give an example to illustrate how this typically goes:

Somebody goes through an unpleasant encounter with someone else and then decides that the entire gender or race of that someone else is one way, and only one way.

That decision is made, a belief is formed and that belief wants to stay, so it'll isolate that somebody into only experiencing realities where that gender or race is that one way while keeping everybody else out of their reality.

Then that person proudly proclaims to have found the truth, without realising they missed a couple of things.

The unpleasant encounter that took place is nothing more than an effect, meaning they could have had some unconscious fears, worries, beliefs, experiences of others or preconceived notions of that gender or race that were simply projected into their reality.

Or there was simply a reshuffle of reality in which they experienced one of many infinite realities that could have been an anomaly, but through their acceptance of it they indicated it to be true, which made it actual so it is now their reality.

This type of belief thrives from reminding you of your experience since truth and experience are one to the ego, merging and deepening its place in your mind.

2. Adoption

The moment others experience something in reality, they experience it as truth; and it is, but only to them until they come and give us the "truth" that we unfortunately accept so it also becomes our truth.

As social creatures, naturally we interact with others without the awareness that consciousness is contagious.

Beliefs are like a virus: they seek to spread themselves around, infiltrating everyone, making them metaphysically contagious. Why? They want to materialise into reality; if not in this person, then maybe the next person.

We may live on one planet, but we don't live in the same world. That's the thing about beliefs: they wish to bring everybody under their umbrella, hence why they want to spread.

Whether its religiously, politically, socioeconomically or even which sports team to follow, each person seeks to spread their beliefs and get more people under the umbrella.

That's the macro-view; on a micro-level, whether consciously or unconsciously, we adopt the beliefs of those around us (friends and family), and those beliefs become invisible to a degree that they are undetectable.

To revert to the example of the unpleasant encounter, what if the person involved is a friend or family member who then shares their story with you?

You may react with shock, dismay, sadness or anger as you empathise and share their pain. The more you think about it, the more upset you become, and without even realising it you adopt their experience as yours.

Then, you have your unpleasant experience with a person who is the same archetype and you tell your friend or family member, solidifying what you both now hold to be true about that gender or race.

Without realising, you unfortunately missed the real truth, which is that truth wasn't yours until you accepted it through the emotion and conviction you invested into it.

Why would we believe something to be true in reality if we haven't experienced it? Simple – we adopted it from those around us.

Don't make the mistake of believing you have been above adopting the beliefs of others. That type of arrogance is coming from the belief itself, which wants to make sure it sticks around so stays invisible through that type of thinking.

This type of belief thrives from reminding you of others' experiences since truth and experience are one to the ego, merging and deepening its place in your mind.

Always remember: your beliefs are either adopted or experienced, or both.

Before you begin adopting new beliefs, you must make the conscious decision that you will no longer believe the things you currently believe.

PRACTICAL

To enter a new reality, you must have a set of new beliefs; any old beliefs will negatively corrupt the frequency of your desired reality and will maintain the old reality.

For example:

You can't believe all rich people are evil devil worshippers and expect to be rich.

You can't believe that you must work hard for money and expect to get money without working hard for it.

You can't believe there are no good men anymore and expect to be in a relationship with a good man.

You can't believe there are no opportunities for people like you and expect opportunities.

Your beliefs must align, contribute to, and support your desired reality. The beliefs must reflect your specific desired reality.

What do you need to believe to easily materialise your desired reality?

You must have the beliefs you'd have in your desired reality now.

Ask yourself this question:

If I was living my desired reality, what would I believe to be true about reality and the world?

Gently meditate upon this question, and know that answers will come because they will, and the moment they do adopt them into your current reality.

I'll help you with some examples:

If you desire a loving relationship, then a belief that is mandatory is that there is an abundance of good men and women everywhere.

If you desire abundance, then a belief that is mandatory is that you always have more than enough.

If you desire a successful business, then a belief that is mandatory is that clients always come to you easily.

If you desire a promotion in your career, then a belief that is mandatory is that you are always seen and appreciated for the work you do.

If you desire to pass an exam, then a belief that is mandatory is that exams are always easy for you.

If you desire money to flow easily to you, then a belief that is mandatory is that you don't have to work hard for money because it always comes to you.

It's simply a game of making sure your beliefs align, reflect, or contribute to your desired reality as opposed to contradict it, which unfortunately is more than often the case.

THERE'S NO CREATION WITHOUT CONVICTION

PRINCIPLE

When creating a new reality, there is no word more important than conviction.

This word is so powerful that it unconsciously creates the desired reality of people who have never even studied reality creation.

There are extremely successful people that will never use a single manifestation technique in their life, let alone read a book on reality creation, but somehow seem to manifest whatever it is they want, and it all comes down to that one word.

Conviction is extreme, unwavering belief in the face of anything; truthfully, it transcends belief into knowing.

Think about it like a big, sturdy tree that stands tall even when the wind blows hard. It's when you believe in something so strongly that you just know it, and just like the tree, you stay firm and don't fall over, even if pushed in a different direction.

Conviction is ultimately the fuel that powers your journey to the destination of your desired reality or an unwanted reality. Unfortunately, the importance of conviction has flown under the radar of the masses while being hidden in the plain sight of religious scriptures.

"And Jesus said unto them, 'Because of your unbelief: for verily I say unto you, If ye have faith as a grain of mustard seed, ye shall say unto this mountain, "Remove hence to yonder place"; and it shall remove; and nothing shall be impossible unto you.'"

Matthew 17:20

It is indeed true that faith can and does move mountains, just not the version of faith by which most of the world are taught to live.

In the modern world, when people speak of faith they are truly referring to trust, and trust will never be enough to alter reality because it indirectly implies the potential for being wrong, which is the breeding ground for doubt.

You trust that people won't betray you, but you only trust because you don't know. Yet knowing is true faith; that is the essence of conviction.

Faith comes from the Latin word *fides*, which referred to a level of confidence that is basically conviction.

It's not about believing; belief is not strong enough to command the forces of nature because, like trust, the only reason we "believe" is because we don't know.

Belief alone will never be enough to alter reality.

You know your name.

You know that when a light switch is flicked, it'll turn on.

You know that when you turn the kettle on, it'll start to boil.

You know these things to such a degree that any attempts to convince yourself otherwise would be dismissed.

You don't believe; you know. True faith is knowing, and realising this awakens the esoteric nature of a multitude of scriptures.

Conviction is the basis of all creation; it empowers the frequency that you put out to the universe, which can either lead to your construction or destruction.

More often than not, we are taught to have conviction in struggle, misery, misfortune, and scarcity; ironically, this strengthens those frequencies, leading to the likelihood of their materialisation.

We strengthen the frequencies of negativity to such a degree that their existence merges itself into what we simply deem as reality, which locks those frequencies into place.

And that's the thing about faith: it doesn't just move mountains; when negatively misdirected, it also creates them as obstacles.

The mountains that we often seek to move are the ones that we have made.

If you could simply cultivate conviction in your desired reality already existing or being inevitable, then your desired reality would simply materialise. It is that simple. With a powerful degree of conviction, techniques wouldn't even be necessary.

How many depend on a manifestation technique? There are millions and millions of videos of people claiming to have the secret technique, when the only secret technique is you; specifically, your conviction.

Without conviction, no technique works. Conviction is what activates the technique to shift you internally, which sets in motion the eventual reflection of that into reality.

What you're able to materialise will always be proportional to the degree of conviction you have surrounding what it is you wish to materialise. The more conviction, the more likely what you want will manifest.

Don't fall into the trap of glorifying conviction as something mystical or unattainable. There's no need to be in awe of it or wonder how to cultivate it. You've already experienced conviction at some point in your life.

There have been moments in your life when you just knew something would happen, whether minor or major; an internal knowing so profound that nothing could convince you otherwise.

Some everyday examples of our convictions:

- I knew I was going to see this person.
- I knew this would happen.
- I knew that they were going to do that.
- I knew that they were going to say that.
- I knew that I was going to get this.
- I knew I was going to get that role.
- I knew that person was going to be mine.
- I knew that person was going to leave me.
- I knew that person was going to cheat on me.
- I knew that I wasn't going to get the job.
- I knew they wouldn't like me.
- I knew I was going to win.
- I knew I was going to lose.

That unshakeable feeling which has come to you before may have felt random, like you didn't know where it came from. But here's the thing: if you did, then you'd be able to flick on conviction like a light switch.

Anyone with complete conviction stands above their reality.

Conviction is like some magical insight that randomly drops from the sky. We have no idea where, when, or why it came, but when it's there, we know it; we feel it, and nothing or no one can convince us otherwise.

The deeper truth is that all conviction you've ever felt or experienced was created and then channelled by and through you.

Think about conviction like a reserve that you have within you that you are unaware of.

Every once in a while, the reserve becomes too full, and it needs to release some of its energy to create space.

When that energy is released, and conviction touches your system, you tap into a frequency so strong that you're able to materialise any idea held in the mind by injecting it with conviction.

That idea can be for or against you, as stated in the examples earlier.

There are a multitude of ideas that exist in your mind, all waiting and seeking to be materialised. When conviction touches the system, those ideas fight for this superpower which make them more likely to materialise.

If the conviction you experience is the result of the reserve being too full, it's natural to wonder how to withdraw from that reserve at will.

Imagine being able to draw from your conviction reserves at any given moment – that's essentially the ability to create your desired reality at any given moment.

So how can we do it?

It's simple. First, you need to understand that the energy of conviction is the second stage of a two-part process. Once you know the energy of the first stage, you'll unlock conviction.

Before conviction is conviction, it is first self-trust.

Self-trust is the first stage of conviction.

Self-trust can be defined as the ability for you to do what you know you need to do, and to avoid doing what you know you shouldn't be doing.

The mind always keeps track; but, more than that, it keeps score of your ability to follow up your own word and your own direction.

There are things that you know you should or need to be doing, but for whatever reason (the old frequency) you're not doing them. This doesn't have to be about creating your desired reality; it's just not about meditating, reading, affirming, or visualising.

It can be as simple as finally going through your emails or letters, updating your CV, going to the gym, cleaning out a room, or standing up for yourself.

The reason it doesn't *necessarily* have to be related to reality creation is because *everything* is related to reality creation; nothing is compartmentalised in the mind.

It's a similar concept to the common adage that how you do one thing is how you do everything; the mind keeps score and records everything.

The more you stick to your word, and the more you follow your own direction, the more self-trust you're going to have, which means, ultimately, the more conviction you're going to have.

As I've said, there are things that you know you shouldn't be doing or don't want to be doing, but for whatever reason (the old frequency) you're doing them. Once again, it can be simple things like not waking up on time, wanting to be punctual but still being late, being quick to judge others, smoking when you've been trying to quit, procrastinating on that thing, or drinking when you've been wanting to stop.

There are indeed spiritual consequences to smoking and drinking, but they do not affect your ability to create your reality. However, if you desire to stop these activities yet you continue to do them, you indirectly deplete your self-trust, which depletes your conviction, which depletes your ability to materialise.

It is not the acts that are the issue but your perception of them.

The erosion of self-trust happens when you repeatedly engage in actions you want to stop but continue doing anyway.

Simultaneously, the more you fail to keep your word, and the more you fail to follow your direction, the less self-trust you're going to have, which means, ultimately, the less conviction you're going to have.

Self-trust is the first reserve that is filled by doing the things you know you should be doing, and it is depleted by doing the things that you know shouldn't be doing. This reserve is then exchanged into the energy of conviction, but it all begins with self-trust.

The more evidence that your mind gathers to prove that you are who you say you are, that you can command and direct yourself, then the more likely reality will believe you when you tell it who you are, and the greater your ability to command reality.

PRACTICAL

Reality creation can sometimes feel like we're on trial, like we're constantly having to defend our desired reality, our thoughts, our feelings and our vision; but, like a trial, the more evidence on your side, the better your case.

The trial is between you and your old frequency: every time that you follow through on your word and the things you know you should or need to be doing, the more evidence for the side of your desired reality.

The more you fail to do what you know you should or need to be doing or, even worse, doing things that you know you shouldn't be doing, the more evidence for the side of your old frequency.

Who's currently winning the trial? Only you know.

The beauty of self-trust is that it highlights something so obvious yet so profound: the only person in the universe that you've ever had to prove anything to is you.

What are those things that you want or need to get done?

What are those things that you want or need to stop doing?

Write them down, no matter how big or small. Remember, there is no big or small to the infinite; it really doesn't matter.

Once defined clearly, now it's a game of discipline.

Unfortunately, this crucial aspect of reality creation is so often overlooked, but there is no getting around it.

How could you ever expect to discipline reality if you can't even discipline yourself? Ironically and metaphysically, you and reality are one, so until you start within you will not change the without.

The first stage is complete, and you've got self-trust locked down. Now it's just a matter of realising that conviction is a muscle that you need to start consciously exercising.

After you've done those things you need to be doing and you start feeling more confident in yourself, that is when it's time to exercise the conviction muscle. Just as with any muscle, the more you use it, the more conditioned it gets.

Exercising the conviction muscle is easy; it's just a matter of you deciding that you know something is going to happen instead of waiting for that feeling to randomly come.

Sounds weird, but that is all there is to it: simply you stating that you know something is going to happen.

It's only weird because, for the most part, conviction has been unconscious to you; but now we are making it conscious, almost like taking breathing off autopilot and making it conscious.

Decide with great precision and unshakeable confidence that you know whatever it is you want to manifest is already yours, and nothing can convince you otherwise.

At first it might feel a bit rough or strange, but that unfamiliar feeling is simply you harnessing the power that, without realising, you've been drip-feeding to yourself your whole life.

To exercise true conviction, you must exercise expectation, because expectation is creation.

Think about the times in your life when you've said, "I knew that was going to happen."

What was that? Did you become a prophet? Did you become a seer?

Every time you "knew," and it happened, you weren't a prophet; you were a creator.

The truth lies in frequency, and the truth is, you created it with a power that's been hidden in plain sight your whole life: you expected it.

Expectancy creates reality.

Expectation is creation.

When you expect something that means you are anticipating it.

Think about a boxer. When he's in the ring, he must anticipate his opponent's punches.

Anticipation is a form of preparation, and to expect is to prepare for the frequency that you are expecting.

When you prepare for something, that means you know it's going to happen, and that's the key that will unlock your desired reality: knowing.

Most people think that manifestation is believing, but, as previously mentioned, that's why they will never manifest; believing isn't enough.

When you believe something, that means it's not a fact. Do you believe that a switch will turn on the light, or do you know it will? That's exactly what expectancy taps into: knowing, confidence and conviction.

Those are the infinity stones of manifestation.

Most live their lives using expectation to create the worst realities for themselves, never realising that through their expectation they are indirectly preparing, opening their arms to their old frequency.

How many times do you expect the worst in life?

Isn't it weird that you expect the worst more than you expect the best? Why? It's almost easier and normal to expect the worst, but why?

It all comes down to programming, conditioning, and training.

The world has trained you to expect the worst, so you create the worst.

Most people expect the worst for two reasons:

1. They've been sold the idea of it.
2. They've experienced it.

Let's look at the first reason. If you want to create your desired reality, then you can't live in *the* world. If you live in *the* world, you will never manifest what you want.

You must live in *your* world.

You need to quite literally create your own bubble and live in it; be consumed by it.

Anything that does not align with your desired reality must be filtered out. People are criticised for being "tone deaf," but that is nothing more than an isolated mind.

I'm not suggesting you act as if the issues of the world do not exist, just to recognise your own issues and prioritise them ahead of those of the world.

The world sells limitation, scarcity, misery, misfortune, and suffering, which when bought sets one up to expect them. It is through that expectancy reality is structured.

Take the concept of recession, for example.

The world will sell you the idea that there will be financial difficulty, unemployment, and layoffs, and it will repeat them until you expect it.

Through training you to expect it, they energetically prepare you to create it.

You get what you expect.

Now let's look at the second reason.

Whenever we go through the worst, to protect our heart we normalise it to avoid the pain of being disappointed or frustrated again. We normalise the worst without realising it as a defence mechanism.

When you normalise the worst, you expect the worst, so you create the worst.

The universe will not seek to alter your perspective. It will simply reflect what you expect, regardless of whether you deserve it or not unfortunately.

To the universe, what you expect is what you are asking for.

It's hard to conceptualise that you may expect the worst, but it's likely you do.

To gauge whether you expect the worst, determine what you find normal.

Do you find it normal to suffer financially? Then you are expecting it.

Do you find it normal for people to let you down? Then you are expecting it.

Do you find it normal to be overlooked at work? Then you are expecting it.

Do you find it normal to unemployed? Then you are expecting it.

Do you find it normal for your business to stagnate? Then you are expecting it.

Whatever you find normal is what you are unconsciously, indirectly expecting, and anything that you find normal will find you.

Your desired reality must become normal to you before it can become normal to the world.

To normalise your desired reality simply requires neutralisation. The moment you become neutral to your desired reality, you collapse the space between you and it.

Neutralisation is simply a matter of relinquishing the external reliance of your desired reality by giving it to yourself internally to such a degree you are good with or without it.

Think about expectation like ordering at a restaurant: if you want steak but you ask for fish, what are they going to bring out?

The direction you look in is eventually where you will find yourself.

A powerful example of faith-based expectancy is found in the biblical story of Elisha and the three kings.

During this time, King Jehoram of Israel, King Jehoshaphat of Judah, and the king of Edom found themselves in a desperate situation. They were preparing for battle against the Moabites, but after marching for seven days, they ran out of water – leaving their armies and animals on the brink of collapse.

In their distress, they sought out the Prophet Elisha for guidance. After consulting the Lord, Elisha gave them a surprising instruction:

"Thus says the Lord: 'Make this valley full of ditches.' For thus says the Lord: 'You shall not see wind, nor shall you see rain; yet that valley shall be filled with water, so that you, your cattle, and your animals may drink.'"

2 Kings 3:16-17

Think about this: there was no visible sign of water, yet Elisha told them to prepare for it anyway. Their act of digging ditches was an expression of faith – taking action before seeing evidence.

And just as God had promised, the next morning, water flowed into the valley from Edom, filling the ditches and providing for their needs. Even more astonishing, the Moabite army, seeing the water in the sunlight, mistook it for blood and assumed their enemies had turned on each other. This led to their defeat, securing victory for Israel.

Prepare even when it is not seen.

This story holds a profound lesson: expectation precedes manifestation. The kings had to act in faith, digging ditches before any sign of water appeared. Likewise, in life, we must often prepare for our blessings before we see physical proof. This is a demonstration of true faith: trusting in the unseen and aligning ourselves with divine provision.

Your current reality may feel like a desert: dry, barren, and hopeless. But just as Elisha instructed the kings to prepare, you too must act in faith, expecting the best even when appearances suggest otherwise.

Dig your ditches; act as if your breakthrough is already on the way.

Release past disappointments; cross the bridge from fear to faith.

Climb the mountain, seek solitude, and elevate your mind above worldly concerns.

Believe it is already done, not by forcing reality to change, but by trusting in the divine timing of provision.

Just as Elisha spoke God's promise and the kings acted accordingly, we are called to trust in the unseen, act in alignment and prepare to receive what is already on its way.

Remember, you get what you expect.

Your life may be currently seem like a desert, but you must elevate yourself if you want to be above the world.

You must expect the best because in doing so you prepare for your desired reality to rain down on you.

You just need to cross the bridge of past resentment, frustration, and disappointment.

Every time you try to expect the best, it is past experiences that hold you back and cause fear within you – fear of disappointment again.

You need to be willing to put your heart out there again while detaching from the necessity of seeing the external world change.

But this time with full conviction that your desired reality will materialise no matter what physical appearances say.

There will be instances your desire does not unfold as intended.

If you have truly manifested, the physical will be irrelevant.

True manifestation is about internally shifting to such a degree you are no longer emotionally dependent on seeing reality change.

To be able to stand in an unwanted reality in a wanted frequency is the beginning of freedom from the slavery of reality.

THE LAW OF EMOTION

PRINCIPLE

> *"There is a piece of flesh in the body if it becomes good (reformed) the whole body becomes good but if it gets spoilt the whole body gets spoilt and that is the heart."*
> ### Sahih al-Bukhari 52

If someone or something can control your emotion, they or it can control your whole reality.

This is not an exaggeration. Ancient wisdom has always stated that "he who makes you mad is your master." This is true not just for the physical but also the metaphysical.

When it comes to manifestation, there seems to be this hyper-fixation on thoughts alone as being the sole contributor to your reality, but a simple reverse engineering of reality reveals otherwise.

If I can control your emotion, I can control your energy in motion.

If I can control your energy in motion, I can control your vibration.

If I can control your vibration, I can control your frequency.

And If I can control your frequency, I can control your reality.

The idea of controlling emotions seems beyond us, and that's because we have been sold the lie that our emotions are out of our control.

Ironically, this belief leads to a frequency where it appears they are, which ultimately leads to a reality that appears out of your control.

It is a paradox that many desire to control their reality but claim they have no control over their emotions.

So long as emotions are out of your control, all attempts at controlling your reality will always appear out of your control.

Emotions only appear to be out of your control because that's how reality also appears. Things happen *to* you as you go through life, cementing the idea that they are outside your control.

You will never get to your desired reality while maintaining the belief that emotions are out of your control.

Emotion is the largest shareholder of your frequency. Its domino effect ripples throughout reality.

Your old frequency will attempt to convince you of the lie that your emotions are out of your control. As it throws adversity at you, you will feel as though you have no choice other than to submit and simply accept the frequency of this adversity.

A side effect of this is emotional turbulence. Unfortunately, this internal turbulence leads to external turbulence.

Emotions themselves also act as glue, sticking you to a frequency, and indirectly a state of reality.

Negative emotions will always glue you to negative conditions, circumstances, events and even people.

Positive emotions will always glue you to the positive conditions, circumstances, events and even people.

If you experience adversity, and as a result experience negative emotions, if not transmuted, those negative emotions will glue you to that adversity, which does nothing more than solidify and strengthen it in your life.

If emotions are the largest shareholder of your frequency, that means your base emotional state, which we call an attitude, is the central unfolding point of your reality.

Attitude is defined as a settled way of thinking or feeling about something.

Your attitude is the emotional baseline that, through repetition, has become ingrained in your identity.

A simple thought experiment that takes a couple of seconds can prove to you that you have always been in your control of your emotions.

Close your eyes and relax. When you feel calm, imagine the person that matters to you the most. See them and allow the love to appear.

Then imagine the idea of being at that person's grave.

Those negative or uncomfortable feelings you just felt were conjured by you. That was you doing it consciously. Most of the time you do it unconsciously, so you don't realise that whether consciously or unconsciously it is still in your control.

The moment you awaken to the truth that you control your emotions, you'll have the entirety of reality in the palm of your hands.

Detach from the idea that they are above you and out of your control, because indirectly this is a confession that reality is out of your control.

Without emotion nothing works. It is the true language of the subconscious mind, and the moment you speak it you will be understood by the universe.

Imagine you only speak Spanish and you encounter someone who only speaks Mandarin. You can spend as much time and effort speaking as you want, but there will be little progression.

That's not to say it will all be in vain. There may be instances of understanding, but it is not ideal nor is it optimal. All miscommunication leads to confusion.

How many miscommunicate with the universe?

When the universe understands you, the materialisation of your desired reality is inevitable; but when it doesn't, the materialisation of your desired reality is a struggle.

Sometimes it can feel like you've done everything you possibly can on your journey to manifesting your desired reality, but still... nothing.

You may have tried multiple manifestation techniques such as affirmations, vision boards, scripting, visualisations, or subliminals, but still... nothing.

Even though you've done the most, you're still getting the least. If you fall into this category, it's because you're not speaking the language of the universe.

The secret to the most powerful and efficient language of the universe lays in the first organ that God gives you when you incarnate on this physical plane: the heart.

Emotion is the true language of the subconscious mind.

It is the gateway to everything you're trying to manifest.

The subconscious mind operates without logic, reason or rationale. It is inherently illogical, much like emotion itself. Emotions don't follow a structured, rational framework; they simply arise and flow.

This shared, irrational nature creates a direct parallel between the two, as both function beyond the realm of conscious reasoning and instead shape reality through feeling and impression rather than analysis.

To control emotion is to control the subconscious.

Think of emotion like the vibrational language through which manifestation occurs, as what is deeply felt becomes frequency which then materialises into reality.

Those who run the world don't require physical force; they simply need to control the emotions of the masses, to control their subconscious minds so they can create their own reality and justify it as truth.

Now, remember, the reality that you are currently experiencing is the result of the frequency you are tuned into.

Think about it like a radio station: each frequency emits a different sound, and reality is no different. Always remember, realities are nothing more than the reflection of their frequency.

Emotion is equal to frequency, and frequency is equal to your reality. Emotions play the largest role in what you experience in reality.

The heart and emotions are the key.

Most people make the mistake of not injecting emotion into their thoughts intended to materialise their desired reality.

Affirmations without emotion are dead.

Visualization without emotion is dead.

Vision boards without emotion are dead.

Positive thinking without emotion is dead.

It is the missing key which will unlock everything that you have been doing. It is what supercharges the frequency of a specific thought, making it more likely to materialise in reality.

Since emotion is the language of the subconscious mind, it is the language of God.

In the teachings of the Bible, the Quran and Ancient Egypt (Khemet), the heart has always been the gateway to eternal life and the consciousness of the infinite intelligence.

The heart is revered in nearly all ancient scriptures and spiritual traditions, yet its deeper esoteric significance is often overshadowed or overlooked in favour of intellectual understanding.

"For as he thinketh in his heart, so is he: Eat and drink, saith he to thee; but his heart is not with thee."

Proverbs 23:7

The verse does not state "For as he thinketh, so is he" but "in his heart", illustrating that thoughts nurtured with emotion lead to one's frequency.

Not all thoughts are made equal; it is not thought alone that leads to creation of one's reality, but the thoughts that are backed by the heart, by emotion.

> *"Keep thy heart with all diligence; for out of it are the issues of life."*
>
> **Proverbs 4:23**

This verse illustrates that the heart must be protected, for the issues that we experience in reality stem from it, and with a metaphysical understanding it all makes sense.

The heart produces emotion.

Emotion is energy in motion.

When energy that is in motion gains momentum, it becomes vibration.

When vibration continues to gain momentum, it becomes frequency.

Frequency is nothing more than immaterialised reality.

The suffering that we often experience can be traced to our hearts, and so ultimately our frequency. Many suffer adversity and let reality hurt or distort their hearts naturally, but unfortunately this leads to a distorted reality.

Everything is a reference to everything you can experience in reality; the origin of reality is your frequency, and a large percentage of your frequency is derived from the heart.

It has been stated that the heart produces an electromagnetic field that is 60 to 100 times larger than that of the brain, highlighting the power of the heart.

In Ancient Egypt (Khemet), it was believed that the heart recorded all the good and bad deeds of a person's life, and was needed for judgment in the afterlife.

PRACTICAL

Your emotional state nourishes and allows your mental state, which can take place either positively or negatively.

The emotional state that you occupy must be reflective of your desired reality, meaning that you must feel how you'd feel in your desired reality, now.

Emotion is not just euphoria, joy, excitement, or happiness.

It can refer to serenity, calm, bliss, accomplishment, or satisfaction.

It isn't necessarily overwhelmingly intense, although it can be; it must simply be as close as possible to how you'd feel in your desired reality.

One way to access the emotional state that you would have in your desired reality is to exist in the mental state that you would have in your desired reality.

The other technique, prescribed earlier, is when you internally, intensely, and vividly experience your desired reality to generate the emotion you would feel. The more you do this, the more emotion you'll generate internally.

It should be noted that the more you experience your desired reality internally, the less you'll desire it externally, since the emotions eventually burn out like fuel. This is perfect.

People often conclude, after learning the power of emotions, that they must ignore negative ones as they will ruin everything.

The truth of reality is that adversity is inescapable.

There will be instances in which reality presents an emotionally-stimulating experience that is negative; there's nothing wrong with feeling negative emotions.

The real issue isn't the emotions themselves; it's the lack of awareness around what they are, what they signify, and how to transmute them. Without that understanding, emotion becomes confusion. With it, emotion becomes power.

Emotions are signposts showing whether you are heading in a direction that is either aligned or misaligned with your desires; they are indicators.

It is common for vehicles to display a flashing symbol on the dashboard when something is wrong; emotions are like those flashing symbols showing whether you are creating a reality that is either aligned or misaligned.

Negative emotions are an indication that you are centralising your consciousness on an aspect of reality that is unwanted. That centralisation of consciousness is typically expressed through either thoughts or focus.

The aim of adversity deployed by the old frequency is singular: to immerse you in the whirlwind of emotional turbulence to such a degree that your frequency alters to be resonant with the adversity. Once internally resonant with the adversity, that sets it in motion to eventually be expressed externally.

It simply wants to energetically consume you like a tornado so that you cannot see anything beyond it.

Think back to a moment of adversity, when your internal state became emotionally turbulent. It's as if your perception narrows. Clarity fades, and it feels like nothing else matters. The emotional intensity clouds your awareness, making it difficult to see beyond the immediate experience.

How often in anger or fury do many claim to "see red"?

A human expression that is deep with esoteric meaning.

It illustrates how emotions lead to the alteration of frequency, and frequency is expressed in humans as our awareness, like a lens. When emotional turbulence is introduced within, the lens is smudged.

Any time you find yourself in a negative emotional state, it's a clear sign that the mind is focused consciously or unconsciously on something undesired, whether it's a past event, a current circumstance or a potential future outcome.

The only true way to move through negative emotions is by engaging in a conscious process that shifts the mental filter distorting the emotional energy, a process known as *emotional alchemy*.

Every unwanted reality or adversity holds within it a hidden energetic polarity that, if uncovered, can begin fuelling the materialisation of your desired reality. It's rarely obvious but often subtle, concealed beneath emotional noise and mental resistance.

But it's always there. No adversity exists without its counterpart; an embedded seed that reflects the very reality you're trying to create. Emotional alchemy is the key to uncovering it.

The process of emotional alchemy can be applied to all negative emotion that arises throughout life:

1. Relax – Sit or lie down in a quiet space and allow your body to fully relax.

2. Bring it to Mind – Gently bring the adversity, whether it's a situation, person or event, into your awareness.

3. Feel Fully – Let yourself experience the full depth of the negative emotion without resistance or avoidance. Stay present with it.

4. Stay Until it Shifts – Remain with the emotion until it begins to soften or dissolve. This may take 20, 30, 60 minutes, or even longer; there's no rush. The key is to stay with the feeling until its intensity naturally begins to fade.

5. Reach Neutrality – Eventually, the emotional charge will fade, and you'll arrive at a neutral state.

6. Extract the Seed – From this place of neutrality, revisit the adversity and search for the hidden seed within it – some perspective or insight that supports your desired reality.

7. Feel the Shift – Focus on that new perspective and allow yourself to feel the positive emotions it brings. Immerse yourself in the uplifted state.

8. Integrate – Once you feel the emotional shift, return to your day, keeping your focus on the positive seed. If your mind drifts back to the negative, gently redirect it.

Emotional alchemy is a highly adaptable technique that can be applied across a wide range of challenging circumstances.

Whether you're facing an empty bank account, an eviction notice, disappointing results, difficult people, or high-stress situations, this process can be extrapolated to any adversity that stimulates negativity within.

Emotional alchemy allows you to alter vibration and, therefore, frequency, through a switch in concentration. It's about changing the emotional charge rather than being consumed by it.

True danger arises when you are so terrified of your negative emotions that you seek to resist them.

Frustration, irritation, anger, sadness, apathy, or disappointment aren't to be repressed; they should be fully felt.

What you resist persists.

It is a mistake to repress or ignore emotions; this line of thinking is associated with toxic positivity, which is a breeding ground for covert negative frequencies to still do damage behind the scenes.

There are many "positive" people in negative realities, simply because they fail to hear the song of negativity frequency quietly playing in the backgrounds of their reality.

The suppression of emotions doesn't eliminate them; it only drives them underground, where they continue to influence frequency.

Negative emotions aren't the issue; the issue is the mental distortion that is colouring the energy of emotion to reflect a particular frequency of negativity.

It's not about ignoring the negative emotion. When emotions are fully felt without resistance or mental distortion, they naturally dissolve into pure awareness, revealing the stillness and clarity that was always underneath.

The stillness of the pure being you are is untouched by the fluctuations of emotion. When one rests in the presence of God's consciousness, emotions arise and dissolve like waves in the ocean; experienced but never binding.

Stillness is the only solution to turbulence.

No adversity has authority over you internally unless you grant it so.

TRANSCEND THE COLLECTIVE

PRINCIPLE

To inherit the beliefs of the collective is to be restricted by the limitations of the collective.

Don't inherit the limitations of others, theirs are not yours.

Detach from the consciousness of the collective or be attached to the realities of the collective.

The act of materialising your desired reality is an act of transcending society, specifically the collective consciousness.

At times, it can feel like no matter how hard you try, the universe itself is resisting your desire for change. But the truth is the universe isn't against you. You are, unconsciously.

It's important to understand that the universe doesn't hate you. It simply prioritises convenience, efficiency, and predictability, even if it sometimes feels otherwise.

This leads to a feeling that the universe is against our desire to change for the better, and that mechanism is called energetic equilibrium.

As a system, the universe prefers balance.

The universe naturally seeks energetic balance and convenience. Once something is calibrated to a certain frequency, it will, for the sake of efficiency, work to maintain that frequency, resisting disruption to preserve stability.

Metaphysically, this energetic equilibrium helps to explain why the rich get richer, and the poor get poorer.

Once the universe has you calibrated to a particular frequency, it'll do everything in its power to maintain you at the level, whether you're prospering or suffering, whether it's what you want or not.

Once a frequency stabilises, it becomes preserved and protected at all costs.

It isn't personal. Like your old frequency, it is a blind intelligence that merely acts impartially.

You are a walking universe, so you too are bound by its laws and mechanics. We also have a form of energetic equilibrium within us.

There exists a collective frequency that seeks to bring people under its umbrella and hold them within its grasp.

Society is simply a collection of individuals, and as a result, a collection of walking universes. A multitude of universes in unison creates a societal universe of some sort.

The societal universe has one purpose, and that is to acquire energetic equilibrium. In humanity, this is expressed through conformity.

In the same way you have your old frequency, society has its own frequency, with its own mind and its own desires. The desires are created by the collective consciousness that will seek to maintain its existence through materialising in the lives of those who adhere to it.

Think of it like a hive mind created from a series of synchronised, collective thought-forms, which once materialised and experienced by an individual will be regarded as truth.

"Truths" are nothing more than ideas pretending to be truth, as stated in the hermetic tradition "all truths are half-truths." Regardless, once accepted they will be experienced.

There are collective ideas that the masses accept as truth without ever realising it is simply something they have subconsciously accepted. Once accepted by the subconscious mind, materialisation follows.

Collective truths are Trojan horses.

They appear to be logical, rational and maybe even sensible, but when looked at from a metaphysical view do not serve you to any degree.

What is the point of maintaining a truth that does not serve you?

What is the point of maintaining a belief that does not serve you?

If what you deem to be true or believe materialises in your reality, does that serve you?

How does the idea that all rich people are evil serve you?

How does the idea that the dating industry is terrible serve you?

How does the idea that because you're a certain race or gender the world will be against you serve you?

How does the idea that there are no opportunities in the world serve you?

All completely reasonable, logical and somewhat sensible truths accepted by society, but if they materialise in your reality how do they benefit you to any degree?

You can't have the same state of consciousness or frequency as those around you and expect your reality to be different.

You can't have the same frequency as the average individual and think that your reality will be an exception. To be an exception in reality, you must be an exception mentally.

Being an exception mentally means not accepting the truths of which the world will attempt to convince you, because when it eventually materialises, you will convince yourself that it is the truth.

Until you are willing to give up everything you've regarded as true, you will continue to experience the same reality, which poses a question: is staying in the comfort zone of past experience and "truths" worth more than creating a new truth, a new experience?

Are you ready to give up the collective beliefs?

That is the only way you'll be detached from the reality of the collective.

PRACTICAL

Pondering whether to detach from collective "truths" triggers the societal hive mind into a state of discomfort, which it then projects onto you.

Do you feel audacious?

Do you feel tone deaf?

Do you feel ignorant?

Do you feel crazy?

Deep down, you know that if you were to disconnect from the collective truths and create your own, you'd be looked at as all the above, and that is what you need to accept.

You cannot become an anomaly while thinking like those around you.

You must make the irrational, rational.

You must make the unrealistic, realistic.

You must make the things that don't make sense, make sense.

Frequency will forever defy rationality.

We live in a world where boundaries are imposed by society on what is possible for people to achieve, yet it seems there are those who don't fit the parameters and achieve the unachievable.

There seem to be talentless musicians who are extremely successful.

There seem to be poor actors who are highly regarded.

Those who are unqualified for a position somehow seem to obtain that very position.

For some people, the rules do not seem to apply, and the truth is they don't. But the deeper truth is that there are no rules other than the ones you accept.

The biggest barrier to materialising your desired reality will be what you regard as "common sense." In other words, your logic.

As humans, what we define as logic or common sense is limited to what we can see in the world around us.

We see through a process that involves reflection and refraction of light, but primarily reflection when it comes to perceiving objects. Visible light reflects off the surface of an object and enters our eyes.

The eyes themselves don't see; they receive this light and convert it into electrical signals via the retina. These signals are then sent to the brain, which interprets them and constructs the image we perceive.

The key point is this: we only see a tiny fraction of what actually exists. Visible light makes up just a small portion of the electromagnetic spectrum, which includes many other frequencies like infrared, ultraviolet, X-rays and radio waves, all of which are invisible to the human eye.

Many live a limited existence by regarding a fraction of reality to be its entire truth. By doing so, they set up themselves up to live by this fraction, which then limits their possibilities.

These people will proudly regard themselves as realistic, as if it's a badge of honour. The truth is, it's a badge of dishonour to their infinite nature within.

To be realistic simply means to define your world by what you can see, which indirectly is a confession of you being limited.

What you and those who accept the same as you deem impossible will be the ceiling you impose on yourselves.

There are no truths in reality other than what the subconscious mind accepts as true.

Your desired reality has collective beliefs that surround it. Identify them, clearly defining them and decide to detach from them.

Everything is simply a decision, and the inability to see that comes from the hive mind that seeks to keep you under its umbrella to extract more energy from you.

To make the impossible, possible, it must first be made possible in the mind.

ATTENTION BEATS INTENTION

PRINCIPLE

When sunlight is concentrated it is powerful enough to start a fire. Do not underestimate the power of concentrated energy; in this instance, concentrated attention.

Concentration is a centralisation of energy, which is a form of creation.

Think about concentration like the water that makes a plant grow: what you feed with focus either flourishes into your desired reality or withers into an unwanted reality.

Reality is nothing more than materialised frequency, frequency is nothing more than vibration that has gained momentum, and vibration is formed by concentration.

Whatever condition, circumstance, or event on which you concentrate will begin to vibrationally resonate with you, eventually compounding into a frequency and then solidifying itself as a reality.

Concentration is like a homing beacon, helping whatever you are concentrating on to come and find you.

The person who concentrates on the devil will be found by it.

The person who concentrates on recession will be found by it

The person who concentrates on difficulty will be found by it.

The person who concentrates on scarcity will be found by it.

The person who concentrates on poverty will be found by it.

What finds you is what you are looking for.

Unfortunately, most people tend to concentrate on struggle, misfortune, scarcity, poverty, and failure and so are found by them.

To concentrate upon what is not wanted is to be found by what is not wanted.

Most people do not realise they are drawing these things towards them by focusing on them.

All your effort to align with the frequency or state of your desired reality can be disrupted by a simple misdirection of your concentration.

It's like pulling out some weeds then sleepwalking into your garden and watering those that remain, only to wake up confused by their growth.

What you focus on, you feed.

Even unconscious attention keeps the unwanted alive. Misdirected concentration is misdirected vibration, which leads to misdirected frequency that inevitably leads to a misdirected reality.

When it comes to concentration, the universe abides by the following:

Attention is alignment.

Your attention determines the frequency with which you align, and your reality will always reflect that frequency, regardless of what you say you want.

It doesn't matter how much you desire success; if your attention is on failure, that's where your vibration is directed, and that's the reality you manifest.

It doesn't matter how much you want to be rich; if you focus on what you lack, you're aligning with the frequency of poverty.

It doesn't matter how much you crave abundance; if your attention is on scarcity, that's what you feed into your field.

It doesn't matter how much you seek peace; if your focus is on chaos, that's the energy you're reinforcing.

Reality doesn't respond to your desires; it responds to your dominant concentration.

Concentration is more powerful than intention.

In the universe, you can't sit in two chairs at once. Those chairs represent frequencies, and you're either in one or the other. The one which is the focus of your concentration will ultimately be where you sit, so as a result where the universe sits with you.

To the universe, concentration is not measured by what you desire but with what your attention resonates, implies, or reflects (meaning matching the emotional or energetic tone):

- If your attention resonates with a particular reality, the universe aligns you with that reality.
- If your focus implies that something is true (even subtly), the universe interprets that implication as instruction and begins moving you toward it.
- If your attention reflects a certain belief or expectation, the universe mirrors it back to you through your experience.

In short, it doesn't matter what you want; what matters is what your attention is affirming.

The universe doesn't respond to desire; it responds to energetic consistency.

Concentration will forever revolve around two polarities in your life: the desired reality and the unwanted reality.

Quite simply, if you can concentrate on your desired reality, whether directly or through things that resonate, reflect, or imply it, you will set in motion its creation at a foundational level.

The issue is that adversity is natural and it temporarily siphons your attention, getting you to concentrate on an unwanted reality.

The same goes for an unwanted reality – if you concentrate on it, whether directly or through things that resonate, reflect, or imply it, you will set in motion its creation at a foundational level.

It is a game of awareness.

If you become aware of which polarity you are feeding, you will know when to switch your concentration away from an unwanted reality to a desired reality.

PREPARE TO BE BAD

PRINCIPLE

Your desire to be a "good" person is the very thing keeping you in a bad reality.

At first, the idea of being a good person may not seem like it has anything to do with materialising your desired reality, but unconsciously they're directly interconnected more than many will ever realise.

The issue with the characteristics of a "good" person is that they are directly opposed to what is required for you to materialise your desired reality. That opposition exists on three levels through what is called a social contract.

Until you are willing to break the social contract, you will continue to be signed up to a reality of misfortune, failure, scarcity, suffering, and disharmony.

People often feel like they're being held back by those around them, and while that perception isn't entirely wrong, it's not the full truth. The reality is, no one can truly hold you back except you.

It's lacking awareness of how you're limiting yourself that creates the illusion that others are the cause.

What appears to be external resistance is often just a reflection of your own internal resistance; external factors are never the cause.

A social contract is the unconscious agreement you've made to gain love, acceptance, and approval by conforming to the expectations and desires of those around you.

As mentioned, they exist on three levels: evolutionary, social, and energetic. These are all interconnected, with the same phenomena taking place on different levels.

Evolutionary:

Your ancestors evolved and survived by sticking together in groups, sharing resources and responsibility when it came to protection.

Humans will forever gravitate to groups one way or another, whether cults, cliques, teams, or religions; it's simply the way the brain evolved.

To your primal brain, a group ensures life, which indirectly and unconsciously means not being part of a group causes death; and it still thinks that.

To the brain, belonging equals survival. When we feel we don't belong it can deeply disturb the psyche, creating emotional instability that, as modern science shows, can cause mental health issues over time.

The thing about belonging is that it requires conforming to the collective, whether physically, mentally or spiritually, so we are accepted.

The default human mind instinctively desires to belong, even to its own detriment; it is unconsciously looking for comfort.

Think about school grades: when most of your friends failed a test or got similar results, it felt oddly comforting. But if you failed while most of them did well, you likely felt embarrassed or ashamed. And if you did exceptionally well while they struggled, you might've even felt guilty.

This reflects the silent social contract: a subconscious pull to match the collective, even at the cost of your own potential.

Whenever we don't belong, we feel discomfort; whenever we don't conform, we mentally and emotionally punish ourselves or are punished by others.

Social:

Before we become autonomous, as babies, we spend most of our time simply observing the adults around us. We begin to learn which behaviours attract love and which ones lead to disapproval or rejection.

You learn quickly that certain behaviours are accepted while others are not.

Whenever you displayed behaviours that were desired, those who raised you gave you love, acceptance and approval.

Without realising it, you became addicted to those feelings, to belonging and to conforming.

It's likely that anytime you did not conform, you were met with hate, rejection, and disapproval in one way or another, which in the depths of your primal brain felt like death.

The irony is that those who raised you have more control over your reality than God or any secret society.

Through the family structure, you were taught that conforming brings rewards of love, acceptance, and approval, while not conforming brings punishments of hate, rejection, and disapproval.

Energetic:

Ideas and beliefs are entities that seek to dominate a person's mind and materialise in their reality.

When the ideas and beliefs of multiple individuals are unified, it creates a collective or hive-like mind.

That group entity or hive-mind is more powerful than any individual entity because it is sustained by the energy of many, which strengthens and fortifies its position.

It seeks to recruit more people under its psychological and energetic roof.

It will then use its hosts to prevent others from leaving.

Think politics, cults, religions, sports teams, and schools of thought.

The hive-mind will distribute love, acceptance, and approval through its hosts, which is felt energetically and socially since it's coming through others.

It wants to do nothing more than spread itself to as many minds as possible, and it has an in-built defence mechanism.

When members wish to leave, it distributes disappointment, rejection, disapproval, and hate through its hosts, which is also felt energetically and socially since it's coming through others.

With a clear understanding of the three levels of social contracts, it's now time to re-examine what it truly means to be a "good" person within this new context.

To most, a good person is someone who:

- we can relate to
- doesn't make other people feel bad
- puts others before themselves, even to their own detriment
- knows their place
- is humble

So it stands to reason that, to most people, having characteristics opposing the above makes you a "bad" person.

When most people think of a bad person, they're not thinking of someone evil or immoral; they're simply thinking of somebody that is different, somebody that isn't like them.

Whether you realise this or not, materialising your desired reality requires you to transcend everything it means to be a "good" person in our society, because otherwise you'll be a "good" person in a bad reality.

You will be different, and you won't be like them.

Of course, I'm not condoning evil or immoral behaviour. This is simply a call to unapologetically accept the differences between you and those around you.

The process of materialising your desired reality will require you to unapologetically break the social contract that you signed on all three levels.

Let's examine how the characteristics of a "good" person prevent you from materialising your desired reality:

Someone we can relate to.

It's likely that people will struggle to relate to you if you materialise your desired reality.

If you want to be like everyone else, you will vibrationally self-sabotage the frequency of your desired reality to avoid the discomfort that comes with being no longer relatable.

Someone who doesn't make other people feel bad.

Materialising your desired reality may lead to those around you feeling diminished, insecure and uncomfortable.

These feelings do not arise because of you but because the perception of you to which they could relate no longer exists.

Others feeling discomfort at your success will lead to you purposely dimming your light to avoid making them feel bad.

You'll vibrationally self-sabotage the frequency of your desired reality by diminishing yourself, becoming insecure and uncomfortable in order to make others feel comfortable.

Someone who puts others before themselves, even to their own detriment.

Materialising your desired reality requires a degree of selfishness by prioritising yourself.

If you put others first, you prioritise their frequency instead of yours, meaning it never accumulates the momentum required to materialise.

Someone who knows their place.

Materialising your desired reality requires changing your status quo and leaving others behind.

If you accept the limitations of your place in their world, you accept the same energetic ceiling as them.

Someone who is humble.

It's likely that materialising your desired reality would require you to be the opposite of humble.

You have to lift yourself – your self-worth, self-confidence, and self-concept – which will be interpreted by others as arrogance or egotistic.

So you avoid lifting yourself, and without realising it you lower yourself.

It's clear now that a "good" person is simply someone that conforms.

Those who conform are loved, accepted, and approved.

Conversely, a "bad" person is simply someone that refuses to conform.

Those who don't conform are hated, rejected, and disapproved.

The materialisation of your desired reality will require you to be hated, rejected and disapproved to some degree.

If you want your desired reality, you must accept all that comes with it.

Often, on a subconscious level, we know all that comes with our desired reality, and we avoid it because we aren't ready.

As mentioned earlier, social contracts have an in-built defence mechanism to maintain conformity: self-sabotage.

You will go to any lengths necessary to be a "good" person, which even includes destroying the frequency of your desired reality.

PRACTICAL

There are two ways to break the social contract once and for all:

1. Unapologetic acceptance

Until you can unapologetically accept that attaining your desired reality will lead to those around you considering you to be a bad person, you'll feel guilty for your success.

And as a result, to avoid that feeling of guilt, you will avoid your success because unconsciously in your mind they are merged.

Out of respect for those around you, you will disrespect yourself.

Do you want the love and approval of those around you if it means you never materialise your desired reality?

If the love and approval of those around you is conditional on never materialising your desired reality, is it truly love and approval?

If those around you do not wish for you to be in your desired reality, then what do they wish for you?

Do they truly love you, or do they only love you if you're the same as them?

Have you worked this hard to stay the same?

You can't feel guilty, or you will unconsciously clip your own wings just to stay on the ground.

You must pursue your desired reality without guilt and realise that reaching it would make you an inspiration to others.

2. Make peace with it

Until you can make peace with being different, every time you conceptualise change (your desired reality) your mind will produce nothing but chaos.

Most don't realise that they are weighing themselves down with the chaos they associate with the transformation they desire. It's like trying to swim holding an anchor.

How will they see me?

What will they think of me?

Will they still love me?

The truth is you won't know until you enter that desired reality, but it's your fear of finding out that is corrupting the frequency.

Make peace with being different, and you will find peace in difference.

Create chaos from being different, and you will find chaos in difference.

THE ENERGETIC CEILING
ON YOUR REALITY

PRINCIPLE

Self-worth is your energetic ceiling determining the limits of what you can materialise in reality.

You can have high aspirations, but with a low self-worth those aspirations will always feel out of reach despite all you do.

How can you materialise something of which you do not feel worthy?

Many do not realise that unconsciously they do not feel deserving of what they desire, and so it never finds them.

If you see yourself as unworthy, how else can the universe see you?

You do not rise to the heights of your desires; you fall to your level of self-worth.

Unconsciously, an individual with low self-worth will not see themselves as worthy of their desired reality. Despite having the right intentions and striving for their desired reality, they have a ceiling above which they cannot go.

It does not matter how much an individual deserves a particular reality; they cannot reach above the level of their self-worth.

The more self-worth you have, the higher the ceiling on what you can materialise and the less you're confined.

The less self-worth you have, the lower the ceiling on what you can materialise and the more you're confined.

Individuals with high self-worth are limitless, while individuals with low self-worth are limited.

The mistake that most make is allowing their self-worth, which is internal, to be determined by the external.

As humans, we typically derive self-worth from others' opinions of us or our successes (worthy) and failures (unworthy).

The universe will never give you more than what you know you deserve.

Self-worth ultimately determines what you know you deserve, not what you believe you deserve; the two are often mistaken.

You may believe you deserve better, yet it doesn't arrive; not because you don't believe it, but because you don't know it.

Self-worth isn't about belief; it's about knowing. Belief lives in the conscious mind, but reality responds to the subconscious, and the subconscious speaks in emotion.

Knowing transcends belief because it's emotional and embodied. The universe reflects not what you consciously believe you deserve, but what you've emotionally experienced.

The most emotionally intense moments, whether positive or negative, imprint the subconscious and define your baseline of worth. This is what sets your frequency or state of consciousness.

An individual can believe they deserve prosperity, but due to their emotionally intense experiences with suffering, their subconscious mind only knows suffering, unfortunately leading to the materialisation of suffering.

An individual can believe they deserve wealth, but due to their emotionally intense experiences with poverty, their subconscious mind only knows poverty, unfortunately leading to the materialisation of poverty.

An individual can believe they deserve a healthy, loving relationship, but due to their emotionally intense experiences with toxic relationships, their subconscious mind only knows toxic relationships, unfortunately leading to the materialisation of toxic relationships.

An individual can believe they deserve abundance, but due to their emotionally intense experiences with scarcity, their subconscious mind only knows scarcity, unfortunately leading to the materialisation of scarcity.

Until your self-worth matches your desired reality, you will vibrationally self-sabotage its materialisation without even knowing it.

To the universe, what you deserve is what you have emotionally experienced.

An individual who desires love but feels undeserving of love will vibrationally self-sabotage whether directly or indirectly, consciously or unconsciously.

An individual who desires respect but feels undeserving of respect will vibrationally self-sabotage whether directly or indirectly, consciously or unconsciously.

An individual who desires appreciation but feels undeserving of appreciation will vibrationally self-sabotage whether directly or indirectly, consciously or unconsciously.

Your frequency speaks before you do.

Knowing is determined by what you have experienced internally, emotionally and intensely.

The epicentre of self-worth is the annoying law of the universe we touched upon earlier: you can only have what you already have.

To deserve better, you must intensely and emotionally know better.

To deserve love, you must intensely and emotionally know love.

To deserve wealth, you must intensely and emotionally know wealth.

Anything you do not know will never grow.

Anything you believe is what you ultimately fail to achieve.

It seems frustrating that what we deserve is what we have experienced intensely and emotionally, especially when we have gone through adversity, pain, and suffering. However, this presents an opportunity.

Since the mind cannot distinguish between reality and imagination, this allows you to alter what you subconsciously know, altering what you think you deserve, which lifts your self-worth, which eventually leads to your energetic ceiling being lifted.

All you need to do is internally cultivate an experience that is so emotionally intense that it becomes real to the mind. By doing so, you can overwrite what you "know," which overwrites what you deserve, which overwrites your self-worth, which overwrites the ceiling.

Until self-worth is detached from the external it will be attached to an illusion, and so long as it is attached to an illusion it will not be grounded in truth.

Self-worth is attached to the external in two main ways:

1. Dependency on others.
2. Dependency on successes and failures.

These two external dependencies are ultimately what shapes self-worth, indirectly shaping the energetic ceiling one has.

Most people live their lives having their self-worth determined by other people.

The more approval, validation and recognition that you get from others, which is the external, the more we feel worthy.

This can come in the form of accolades, compliments or approval from others, which have the ability to either increase or decrease your self-worth.

If others can increase or decrease your self-worth, then they are controlling your frequency, ultimately controlling your reality. Many fail to realise this.

Self-worth is an energetic ceiling: if people possess the power to determine your self-worth, they determine the limits of what you can materialise in reality.

How many allow their self-worth to be dependent on others?

"Care about what other people think, and you will always be their prisoner."
Lao Tzu

The idea of "not caring what people think" is often seen in a negative light, but that's a misunderstanding.

Whether positively or negatively affected, a door is opened.

True freedom means being unattached to both their criticism and their praise.

To detach from your self-worth being dependent on others, you must realise that nobody will ever see the real you.

The idea of being emotionally swayed by what others think is pointless if you understand the nature of reality. Understand that people don't see you as you are; they see you as they are. Even when they try hard, they're not seeing you; they're seeing you through their own frequency, their own tinted lens.

Alternatively, nobody cannot see you beyond their preconceived notion of you. Ultimately, their minds will filter out and dismiss anything that does not align with that preconceived of notion of you.

What people think is based on where they are vibrationally, and if they aren't in a vibration that you wish to be compounded into frequency then materialised as reality, why do you care?

Validation and approval aren't the issue; the issue is the external reliance on them.

PRACTICAL

The moment you become internally reliant, you become independent of reality. This is true freedom: to be free from reality dictating your internal self.

Validation and approval must come from within, and only within.

You must use your imagination to cultivate an internal experience that intensely stimulates feelings of approval and validation.

That can be a scene or the sounds of people praising you, appreciating you, honouring and respecting you. Use the technique prescribed.

In doing so, you detach from external reliance, and you alter what you know, altering what you deserve and ultimately what you're able to materialise.

Seeking validation and approval from others means you lack it from yourself. Through utilising the mind to create experiences in which you are validated and approved of within, you set in motion for it to materialise without.

What you desire from the world is what you must give yourself before the world gives it to you.

Moving on to successes and failures, the other way in which we derive our self-worth.

To adhere to the concept of success and failure is to unconsciously and vibrationally subject yourself to the illusion of polarity. The mind that sees two instead of one is separated, and to be separated internally is to be separated externally.

Success can prompt intense feelings of pleasure, accomplishment, and satisfaction, which seems harmless. But by allowing the external to take you to the heights of happiness, you unknowingly open the door for it to take you down to the lows of sadness.

Failure can prompt intense feelings of pain, disappointment, and dissatisfaction.

The heights of pleasure and the lows of displeasure.

The heights of euphoria and the lows of dysphoria.

Without realising it, you have made your internal dependent on the external.

Without realising it, you have empowered the external and made yourself powerless.

Without realising it, you have now subjected yourself to reality's emotional rollercoaster, rising high whenever it desires positive energy or plunging low when it desires negative energy.

You need to transcend seeing life as a series of successes and failures.

Detach from those labels, and you will energetically detach from the vibratory effects of those labels.

Through labelling reality, we attribute meaning; when we attribute meaning, we attribute emotion; when we attribute emotion, we attribute frequency; when we attribute frequency, we attribute reality.

Labels are part of our perception, which ultimately leads to our projection; and to perceive something as lost is to project the meaning (emotion) of loss into your reality.

When loss causes your self-worth to take a hit, that is only due to the meaning that you have attributed to that loss. Over time, if consistently repeated, this leads to our self-worth diminishing.

There are no wins and losses, everything is one.

There are no successes and failures, everything is one.

Categorising some things as wins and others as losses is the source of your separation, which is the source of your limitation.

See everything you experience as a win and only a win.

By doing so, you transcend the duality of losses, the meaning of losses, the emotions of losses, the perception of losses and, finally, the projection of losses.

You only perceive a win, so inevitability all conditions, circumstances and events of reality only project a win.

To label loss is to create a detour from your desired reality.

When you awaken to the truth that all paths on the journey to your desired reality are created by you, then you stop creating multiple paths and only follow one. Reaching your destination becomes not just possible, but inevitable.

When you are the source of your self-worth, the world can never take anything from you.

WHAT TO DO WHEN REALITY GOES WRONG

PRACTICAL

Adversity is guaranteed in reality.

There will be times when, despite all your efforts, reality feels heavy; like everything is going wrong and the world is against you.

There will be times when it feels like nothing that you are doing is working.

There will be times you question your ability to change your reality.

Adversity is inescapable, but that does not make it the be all and end all; how you deal with the frequent lows of reality is true alchemy.

How you respond to reality going "wrong" determines whether you reinforce your old reality or solidify the new one. In moments of adversity, we often unconsciously slip back into the old frequency, unknowingly reinforcing the very reality we're trying to leave behind.

There are four ways to deal with adversity. Keeping them in your arsenal will prevent the destruction of the frequency of your desired reality.

1. Give Yourself Grace

You have been asleep much longer than you have been awake.

You've spent more time in the frequency of your old world, being asleep, than you have being awakened.

This means that the strength of the old frequency is more solidified and momentarily stronger than the new frequency into which you're currently trying to shift.

It's likely that you've spent more years of your life without this knowledge than with it, and remembering this is the path to giving yourself grace.

Mistakenly, as you begin to expand your consciousness and become aware of the mechanics of the universe, it can lead to your old frequency setting a trap...

And that is to set you up with the desire to strive for perfection and excellence all the time. It does this because it knows you can't achieve this so eventually, when you fail, you'll descend into the very same emotions it feeds on.

How do you feel when things are going wrong? Hopeless? Frustrated? Irritated? Confused? Apathetic?

These are the very emotions feeding your old frequency. They're its fuel source, keeping it alive and active. The moment you descend into the negative emotions that it desires, you no longer see clearly.

Without a proper perspective, you'll feel guilty at every stumble, negatively altering the frequency you emit.

Without a proper perspective, you'll feel annoyed at every stumble negatively altering the frequency you emit.

Without a proper perspective, you'll feel frustrated at every stumble negatively altering the frequency you emit.

Without a proper perspective, you'll feel hopeless at every stumble negatively altering the frequency you emit.

The old frequency wants to make you feel like you've let yourself down. You feel like you've let down your desired reality and that all your work is ruined.

Your progression towards your desired reality can never be lost; the only loss is in the belief of your desired frequency already existing.

People often spiral when they slip, thinking they've gone back to square one. But the truth is, you only return to square one if you decide you're back there. It's not the slip that resets you; it's the meaning you give it.

It's a scam. Before Ponzi, there were entities.

You fail, you feel guilty, and then that guilt consumes you, drowns you, and without even realizing it, time has passed and you're back in your old ways.

Until you know what I'm about to tell you, you'll continue to fall for this scam. So listen up: I'm sorry to break it to you, but you can't be high frequency all the time.

One of the most misleading aspects of the spiritual community is its overemphasis on being "high frequency" or "high vibrational." Ironically, it's this very fixation that often keeps people stuck in so-called "lower" states.

Trying to be on a higher frequency all the time will cause you to be on a lower frequency.

Frequency is simply a level of awareness. To be in a higher frequency isn't about feeling good or euphoric although that is a side of effect of having a higher level of awareness.

To be in a "low" frequency is to have a low level of awareness; the lens through which you see reality is distorted and blurred by you.

Frequencies are forever oscillating.

Up.

Down.

Up.

Down.

This is the nature of the universe. So why do you think you can fight it?

Frequencies aren't still; they're always moving, even if ever so slightly. The truth is, you falling back into your old frequency is completely normal.

In fact, it's forever going to happen.

As you know, you can't have high without low, and light without dark.

So why are you shocked you've fallen? Did you not rise first?

This is the nature of the universe.

The ancient alchemists referred to this as the Law of Rhythm.

"Everything flows, out and in; everything has its tides; all things rise and fall; the pendulum-swing manifests in everything; the measure of the swing to the right is the measure of the swing to the left; rhythm compensates."

The Kybalion

All things rise and fall.

The measure of the swing to the right is the measure of the swing to the left.

Falling back into your old ways is part of the universe.

The issue is, you're trying to fight a tide, and you can't.

Being frustrated with falling back into your old patterns is like being upset that night turns to day.

You're striving for something that doesn't exist and isn't attainable. Once again, you're being set up.

Once you recognise that falling back into your old frequency is simply part of the ebbs and flows of the universe, you'll be in a position to actually transmute it.

You're not going to be disappointed every time you have a slip in frequency because it's normal.

You can't rise without a drop; you can't have higher without the lower.

The first step to getting back into your new frequency is freeing yourself from the frustration and guilt.

Frustration and guilt bind you to your old frequency; they are a poisonous glue that destroys you.

The more you resist, the more they persist.

The only reason you've fallen is because you've risen.

While you're wallowing in self-pity, guilt, and frustration, those emotions blind you and make you forget that you rose to begin with.

You couldn't have fallen back into your old frequency if you hadn't risen out of it, which means you can do it again.

This revelation can give you the confidence and empowerment to disrupt the negative emotions that are currently clouding you.

The mistake most people make when they fall back into their old frequency is focusing on their "failure."

This feeds their old frequency, which becomes stronger; they fail to realise they could have just fed the new frequency instead.

Feeding the new frequency is so simple: just focus on your past wins.

This will tap you into the frequency you had while you were rising. This energy can never be destroyed, as it exists within, so you will always be able to return to it.

It all begins with your concentration.

Whether you realise this or not, you've been focusing on what you don't want to experience, consciously or unconsciously.

As a result, your concentration has altered your vibration, altering what you experience in reality. You need to stop concentrating on your fall and concentrate on your rise.

The moment you release the guilt, frustration, and irritation you believe you deserve to feel, you stop feeding the old frequency.

That emotional weight does nothing but reinforce what you're trying to move beyond. Recognizing this is the prerequisite to three key steps you must take when reality feels like it's falling apart.

How did you feel when you rose?

How do you feel when you think about how much you elevated yourself?

Immerse yourself these feelings and let them marinate.

The inability to see your rise isn't a confession that you have not risen, but an indication that the old frequency has clouded your consciousness.

You just need to give yourself permission to feel that pride, confidence, and self-accomplishment.

Feel it all, because that is the fuel that'll take you back to your desired reality.

1. Transcend the label of "wrong"

Things only go wrong because you adhere to the illusion of wrong.

Reality will only ever be unmovable to the degree that you are unmovable, and you need to rid yourself of adhering to the concept of "wrong."

Do not forget, since there are no truths in reality other than what the subconscious mind accepts as true, you make the laws of your reality based upon your conviction behind a belief.

Once you start to internalise the idea that reality is wrong or things aren't working, you set in motion a frequency that moulds your reality to reflect that idea, which is strengthened by the emotions behind it – usually frustration, irritation, annoyance, anger, or sadness.

When it comes to your desired reality, reality can never go wrong.

Eradicate the concept of "wrong" from your vocabulary to eradicate it from your reality.

What we deem to be right or wrong in our reality is nothing more than the illusionary law of polarity in operation.

Energetic pairs such as masculine and feminine, negative and positive or good and bad only appear to be separate in our third-dimensional realm; outside of our reality, on a quantum level, everything is one.

There is no separation outside of our reality, from where you must materialise your desired reality; meaning you must be above the polarity of reality and begin seeing everything as one.

This extends to labelling reality. Everything in reality simply "is."

The inability to see this is due to our desire to moralise the universe, which will result in nothing more than pain and frustration.

The universe doesn't adhere to morality; gravity acts upon the innocent child in the same manner as it does an evil adult.

How would you feel if you knew that nothing can ever truly go wrong in your reality?

That despite how things appear temporarily, everything is leading to one place?

Traditionally, our concept of things going right or wrong stems from the idea of God (right) and the devil (wrong).

Many assume the devil must exist because they believe God, like everything else in reality, something must have an opposite. But this reasoning overlooks a key truth:

God exists beyond this reality and therefore beyond polarity.

God is not bound by duality, contrast, or opposites. So if God is above polarity, then God has no true opposition, meaning the concept of the devil as God's equal opposite is a misunderstanding.

There is only one power in the universe, and that is God.

As it is often said: the devil is a lie.

The concept of the devil is rooted in the belief that things can go wrong: that you can stray, take the wrong path, or fall into darkness. But when that darkness is illuminated by the light of truth, the illusion of multiple conflicting paths dissolves, revealing that there was only ever one true path all along.

This isn't about debating the existence or validity of the devil, but rather bringing awareness to a deeper truth: there is ultimately only one power in the universe, expressing itself through different vibrational states.

Never forget that whatever you experience in reality, so long as you maintain the idea that all paths lead to one place, every apparent change in direction will simply be another route to the same location.

There are no detours, unless you create them through the idea that things can go wrong.

Look at the "wrongs" of your reality as a delayed form of consciousness, making their way out to create space for your desired reality, as opposed to an indication that they still exist and have power over you.

2. Alter how you look at life, and life will alter the way it looks at you

Your perception is being used against you, and until it serves you it will destroy you.

The alchemist takes advantage of the fact that life is meaningless.

That does not mean that life is valueless, but the meaning that we attribute to reality is just that, what we attribute.

The label or meaning you attribute to reality will ultimately alter your reality to reflect the energy behind that label.

If you see everything as going wrong, then everything energetically within that label will imprint itself onto your reality, altering it to reflect everything that is aligned with wrong.

Until you can redefine the experiences of reality to serve you, reality will control you.

To truly alchemise your reality, see everything going wrong as sign that everything is going right.

Remember, the only difference between things going well for you and things going badly for you is the rate of vibration.

Your vibration is preceded by your concentration. If you continuously focus on the aspects of your reality which are going wrong, that concentration will be reflected in your vibration, which will gain momentum until it becomes a frequency, and every frequency must turn into a reality.

Alternatively, if you consistently focus on the parts of your reality where everything is going right, with enough momentum this vibration becomes your dominant frequency.

You can have good intentions in your reality, but ultimately your concentration is more powerful than your intention.

3. Stand calmly among the chaos

The world can only give you what you give yourself first.

To truly alter your world, you must be whatever you desire before the world proves it to you because it will never prove what you are already not.

Sometimes life can be chaotic; it can feel as though everything terrible is happening at once, and it is choking you.

The only way out of the chaos in your external reality is through cultivating peace internally. You need to be able to stand calmly among the chaos.

The chaos will remain so long as it exists internally, but once removed and dissolved, eventually it has no choice but to do the same externally too.

In some instances, it can feel as though we are powerless over reality and the conditions, circumstances, events, and even people around us have more power than us. But you can regain your power with one realisation...

The power creating the chaos that's getting you down, is owned by you. It has simply been externalised.

The strength of the chaos is fuelled by you.

The power of that chaos doesn't belong to the external; it belongs to you.

Any control the external has over you is only what you give it.

The same strength of that chaos can be redirected to peace. It has no power or strength over you except what it borrows from you.

You're projecting your power onto the chaos, thinking it is strong. No, it is you that is strong, and you always have been.

You can redirect that same strength towards peace rather than chaos.

The waves outside of you can only be brought to stillness by the stillness inside of you.

It's worth reiterating here that the notion of things not working or going wrong is a confession of misalignment with the true essence of manifestation.

Manifestation is internally shifting to a degree to which you are no longer emotionally dependent on seeing reality change.

Things not working is an admission that you have not shifted internally to such a degree that your mind has accepted your desired reality.

OUTRO

You now know more than enough.

You'll return to these pages. And when you do, you won't be the same.

What was once hidden will now be obvious not because the words have changed, but because *you* have.

This book is you. As you evolve, it evolves with you.

With everything within these pages, you now have what you need to outsmart your old frequency and by doing so, outsmart reality itself.

There will be moments when you forget this knowledge and that's okay.

This isn't about being perfect.

It's about remembering more often.

The more you consciously bring this awareness to the top of your mind, the more you'll find yourself naturally staying above the noise effortlessly staying on top of your reality.

There will be times when reality seems one step ahead of you. When that happens, don't panic. Just come back.

Come back to your knowing. Come back to the frequency of having. Come back to yourself.

It's never about what's going to happen, it's about who you're going to be when it does happen.

Do not ever let the world gaslight you into believing that causality exists in external circumstances.

You are and always will be one with the source.

The moment you start attributing your outcomes to money, business strategies, other people, or fleeting opportunities, you fall into the grand illusion. You begin to worship false gods mistaking the mirror for the cause, when it has only ever been the reflection of your internal state.

Money is not the source of abundance.

Business tactics are not the source of success.

No person is the source of your love, validation, or fulfilment.

And external achievements are never the source of your worth.

All of these are effects shadows cast by the light of your own consciousness.

When you believe that anything *out there* holds power over your reality, you hand over your throne. You become a servant to the very illusions you were born to command.

Remember:

It is not the market, the economy, the algorithm, the client, the partner, or the timing.

It is *you*. It has only ever been you.

The world will constantly try to convince you otherwise. It will point to evidence, logic, and consensus to prove that you are at the mercy of external forces.

Do not fall for it.

Refuse to make idols out of effects. Refuse to forget that the true cause the only cause is within you.

When you reclaim that truth, money flows, relationships align, success unfolds not because they *gave* you anything, but because you stopped chasing shadows and stood as the source.

The only true thing that exists in this universe is consciousness, that is all you have and all you will ever need.

Now go and outsmart reality.

Made in the USA
Las Vegas, NV
06 July 2025

24406982R00144